JEWS ARE THE PROBLEM

Ayo H. Kimathi

JEWS ARE THE PROBLEM

Ayo H. Kimathi

ISBN 9781948323208
Second edition

For speaking engagements, book signings, or other inquiries, contact us at: *truth@jewsaretheproblem.com*

Manufactured in the United States of America by

MONEY TREE PUBLISHING

MONEY TREE PUBLISHING
6256 Bullet Drive
Crestview • Florida • 32536
(850) 689-8989
moneytreepublishing.com

TABLE OF CONTENTS

"Controlling the world's sources of news, Jews can always prepare the minds of people for their next move. The greatest exposure yet to be made is the way the news is manufactured and in the way the whole world is molded for a purpose. When the powerful Jew is at last traced and his hand revealed, then comes the ready cry of persecution, and it echoes through the world press. The real causes of persecution (which is the oppression of the people by the financial practices of Jews) are never given publicity."
—Henry Ford Sr. (May 1920)

"You know, I think you're a Jew with an Anglicized name. His involuntary expression told me I'd hit the button . . . But I said at the same time I knew that the Jew played these roles for a very careful strategic reason: the more prejudice in America could be focused upon the Negro, then the more the white Gentiles' prejudice would keep diverted off the Jew."
—Malcolm X (1965)

"Ye are of your father the devil, and the lusts of your father ye will do. He was a murderer from the beginning, and abode not in the truth, because there is no truth in him. When he speaketh a lie, he speaketh of his own: for he is a liar, and the father of it."
—Jesus Christ (John 8:44 KJV)

A Note From Andy Hitchcock . . .

In 2006, I wrote a book entitled, *The Synagogue of Satan*, based upon what I had learnt via my own historical research, that conflicted in so many ways with the mainstream historical narrative, but made far more sense than the mainstream historical narrative ever had.

Some months ago, my publisher, David Gahary, made me aware of a book written by Ayo Kimathi, entitled, *Jews Are The Problem*.

As soon as I heard the title, I was both engaged and dismayed. Engaged by the fact that Ayo was clearly tackling what I interpreted to be the subject of Jewish Power, and dismayed by the fact that the so-called hate speech laws in the UK, where I am based, would prevent me from even having the temerity to quote the title of the book, never mind inviting Ayo onto my Internet radio show to discuss his book.

On that basis, I politely declined David's offer of a free copy of the book to review back then, and when he approached me recently to write something for the second edition of this book, I agreed to do so on the condition that I not read the book beforehand.

How can you write something for a book you have never read, you may ask?

Well, very simply, I can tell you what I am aware of from the book that I have heard the author present on several Internet radio shows that I listen to, broadcast out of the USA. These were presented by my good friend Giuseppe Vafanculo, and I am aware that another couple of friends of mine, Handsome Truth and Jim Rizoli, also interviewed Ayo on their respective shows, but guess what, I couldn't listen to those, as the BitChute channel they were published on was blocked in the UK as a result of what they determine to be "hate speech."

What struck me about Ayo's interviews with Giuseppe, is that whilst I was aware of much of the history to which he referred, he also brought up other elements of history I was unaware of, and went beyond what I considered a historical event I knew all about.

My primary memory of this is the 1913 Leo Frank trial on the murder and rape of the 13-year-old girl Mary Phagan. Whilst I believed I knew all I needed to know on this subject, Ayo pointed out something I was completely unaware of.

Whilst I knew that Leo Frank tried to blame the rape and murder of little Mary Phagan on Jim Colney, a Black man, I did not know that the 1915 film, *The Birth of a Nation*, essentially ran with that lie, a lie that was proven to be a lie in court, and a lie which Ayo quite understandably believes, resulted in the conflict between American Blacks and Whites during the 20th century.

In conclusion, I say this. If you value your First Amendment right to free speech then DEFEND IT! However, if you don't value it, and are instead content to live in a country where one historian cannot interview another historian, purely due to the title of his book, never mind the content, then do nothing.

The choice is yours.

Andrew Carrington Hitchcock
January 9, 2023

FOREWORD

Even though race is a man-made construct, the race problem is beyond Black and White. It is a construct that pits Whites against Whites with Blacks caught in the middle. We have seen this played out in many historical scenarios. We witnessed this beginning in the 15th century when European countries began to colonize Afrika in a mad scramble to rape and control her resources. We saw this being played out with fierce competition amongst the Dutch and British for control of the diamond mines and land in South Africa during the Boer wars. At the conclusion of these wars, the Jewish family De Beers would control the mines of South Africa—courtesy of cheap Black South African labor coupled with Dutch and British enmity.

The Afrikan/Atlantic enslavement trade continued to exploit Afrikan labor as Europe transitioned from feudalism to capitalism. For control of the colonial North American territory and to usher in Afrikan slave commerce, France and Britain engaged in a warfare contest. Once again, we see Jewish participation. Tony Martin's book *The Jewish Onslaught* documents the financing of slave ships by Jews used to transport the Afrikan to the American enslavement horror.

It is against this backdrop Ayo Kimathi's book, *Jews Are The Problem,* clearly demonstrates and connects the dots to the clandestine Jewish participation in undermining Black liberation and freedom struggles. Kimathi uses significant historical moments in the Black struggle to evince the surreptitious machinations employed by Jews. From the Compromise of 1877, which ultimately decimated Black Reconstruction, to the movie, *The Birth of a Nation,* which unleashed the KKK on Blacks, accelerating "strange fruit" hanging from poplar trees, to the stereotypes created by Hollywood which have relegated us to toms, coons, bucks, and buffoons, Kimathi convincingly documents how the spokes in the wheel lead to the Jewish hub. At the same time, many White nationalist organizations castigate Jews for their control of banking, media, and movies. In response, Jews offer up Blacks as cannon fodder resulting in racial animus. The confusion you once held about this issue has been deconstructed. Kimathi has given us, with laser-like focus, the coordinates for our freedom.

Brother Olodumare

PREFACE

Henry Ford was right. The International Jew is the world's foremost problem. And as of March 2022, they are a few steps away from their centuries-old agenda of mass exterminating the world's population and enslaving any non-Jews who survive (aka Gentiles or *goyim*).

If not for their egotism and incorrigible approach to slavery and genocide, they would possibly accomplish their objectives without much resistance. However, their arrogance has awakened enough men and women who aren't cowards, that their objective to exterminate us will likely boomerang around to them. If this occurs, the Jew will not survive the 21st century.

If the global extermination of non-Jews was not staring us directly in the eyes, most people would immediately put this book down and stop reading it. However, anyone reading this book is witnessing pedophilia in children's books at their local libraries or elementary schools, daily deaths from people who've taken the harmful injections falsely classified as "vaccinations" (that don't vaccinate), homosexuality and perversion spread throughout all forms of media, censorship on a level never before experienced by the American public, strategically planned and executed economic ruin of a wealthy nation, organized child sex-trafficking rings run by the leaders of nations, systematic premeditated murder in hospitals using treatable illnesses as the pretext, government-sponsored sabotage to a nation's food supply, overt economic terrorism through forced unemployment and money control, racial manipulation and incitement ping pong, organized overthrows of sovereign nations, destruction of presidents who won't comply with Israel or the

West's desires (Lesbians, Gays, Bisexuals, & Transgenders (LGBT) acceptance, North Atlantic Treaty Organization (NATO) demands, forced injections), forced technology injections into men, women, and children, unnecessary and undesired military wars throughout the world, etc.

All of these calamities and more are being spearheaded by the Jews. Those who can see it, know it. Those who know it and can see past their fear, acknowledge it to themselves. Those who acknowledge it to themselves and aren't cowards, share this truth with others. Those who share this truth with others, discuss what can be done to stop these monsters from destroying the planet and its inhabitants.

And then there's me. I walk boldly, publicly, and unabashedly forward to the world and pronounce:

JEWS ARE THE PROBLEM!

1

INTRODUCTION, PURPOSE, APPROACH

Jews Are The Problem. Informed serious people know it; but they will not say it publicly. Many people have an idea of it; but they dare not mention it aloud at the threat of losing their livelihood.

And who wants the political and media backlash that comes with any criticism of this evil group of tyrants? No one. The Jewish reactionary instinct to attack any persons shining light on their nefarious and harmful behavior is notorious. Just consider how they've attacked Ye (formerly Kanye West), Kyrie Irving, and Steve Nash since the first edition of this book.

The reason I am writing this book is because the "Jews Are The Problem." They are the reason for the world's economic crises. They are the catalyst for the world's moral crises. The same can be said for the global censorship crisis, food and fuel shortages, education crisis, mass unemployment, desocialization of society, child sex-trafficking, illegal organ harvesting, pornography and media, perversion and homophilia (homosexuality and pedophilia), promotion and growth of organized Satanism, broken families, chemical/biological injection genocide-to-slavery wars, international lockdowns, male-female relationship strife, global military operations and the destabilization of sovereignty wars, etc.

This book began as a desperate measure to alert the world to pending doom at the hands of the Jews and has quickly turned into the first of a series of books with the same title. Each addition will include a subtitle that describes the perspective that book will address. In each addition, we will discuss the relevant impact of the last book, changes in the world situation, and how well we addressed the genocidal aims of the International Jew. Whatever critical information, assessments, or perspectives don't make it into this book will be material for future additions. In the future, we intend to partner with experts on the International Jew from around the world to provide their contributions. Stay tuned.

Since it is obvious that they are the primary party responsible for the horror of the planet's condition, I am going to do what no one else in the modern context will do. I am going to plainly identify them as the world's foremost problem, explain how they operate, discuss their genocidal escapades, and call for all other parties to put our differences aside until we systematically eliminate this threat. I will even suggest strategies for the world to implement in order to reach this resolution in time for us to avoid our own exterminations.

There are many books that credibly document relevant history of the Jews and their genocidal and brutal behavior throughout the centuries. As a result, I am not going to spend significant time performing scholastic recaps of that which is available to the public. Rather, I will provide Quick Response (QR) codes that will take you to reputable sources to validate different points throughout this discussion. Some codes will link to books, PDFs available for download online, free videos for online viewing, videos for purchase from various sources, or other relevant forms of validation. In this way, you will have the option of pausing at your discretion to get validation and/or visual documentation of points being made. Hopefully, this will provide a 21st century approach to scholarship that incorporates modern technology into the learning process. **I always aim to be the thought leader in addressing topics that people don't see or won't touch, in a way that revolutionizes the information delivery process.** I thank my good friend Ahmose for suggesting QR Codes. He has turned an exciting ride into an exhilarating adventure.

I also chose this process because seeing is believing. And some of the atrocities committed by the Jews are so horrific and disdainful that only visuals can properly capture their essence. For instance, to really digest the horror of the Bolshevik Revolution (Jewish Genocide on Eastern Europeans), one would benefit greatly from watching a video like *Europa*. This 12-hour video can be watched online on *bitchute.com/video/s1nPYDj7KBEQ*:

It is also broken into 10 parts on the same site:

Europa **Part 1**
bitchute.com/video/QtLvxZ9d0yEY

Of course, like every form of media, one has to use discernment and understand that people tell stories from their point of reference. Nevertheless, this is the best source I've ever come across in documenting and showing the horror of Jewish terrorism. In fact, watching what the Jews put the Russian and German people through made me gain a new understanding of White suffering. As an Afrikan in America, I view Whites from my own historical vantage point—as oppressors. I actually watched *Europa* and realized that Jews will exploit, terrorize, and slaughter anybody—no matter the race or religion. And they won't give any mercy. I always knew this theoretically through historical analysis; but nothing I've ever read affected me like *Europa*.

I'm trying to help the blind to see and the scared to realize that not identifying the source of our collective misery is far more frightening than identifying the Jews as **The Problem**. They aren't the only problem; but if we don't wake up and act quickly, we will become victims of the 21st century Bolsheviks (explained later in the book). The Bolsheviks torture and exterminate. If they win, we'll have no further issues to consider—*none of us*.

I'll deploy a common analogy I use to describe what the world is dealing with. Imagine . . .

We have a fleet of 20 ships sailing the seas. We sail in a tight formation, close enough to throw a rock and connect squarely. All of a sudden, something latches onto one of our ships and pulls it under water. Then it happens to another ship. It keeps happening and we all begin to panic. The thing looks like a long snake with suction cups on the end of it. As we're witnessing one ship being attacked by the snake-like thing, we begin to shoot at it. As it appears to be losing a grip on one ship due to our cannon strikes, two similar looking snakes attack two other ships.

At this point, we are trying to figure out what is going on and where these snakes with suction cups are coming from. Fortunately, one of the men on our ship says, "I think I know what this is." We demanded a quick answer. He said, "It's an octopus." We said, "What the @#$%& is an octopus?" He said, "It's a creature with eight legs and a big head that controls all of its tentacles. I mean those things that are pulling our ships down. They're called tentacles." We cried, "What do we do?" He said, "Sail the ships as far apart as possible. Each of these legs are attached to his head. He can't be but so big. If we spread out, he can't get all of us." We instructed all ships to go in different directions until we regrouped to strategize.

Once we got to safety, we called in a submarine to find its location. Once we located this gigantic octopus, we sent a team down and blew his head off. That was the last time we had any issues with that octopus.

This analogy is very similar to the crisis the world finds itself in today:

1) COVID-19 pandemic
2) International lockdowns and business closures
3) Skyrocketing gas prices
4) Massive unemployment
5) Mask mandates
6) Injection mandates (called vaccine mandates)
7) Crashing of the dollar
8) Food shortages
9) World War III (WWIII) pending w/Russia defending itself against NATO

10) Homophilia (homosexuality and pedophilia) promoted everywhere
11) Media censorship
12) Child sex-trafficking
13) Organ trafficking
14) Election corruption
15) Overthrow of the Republic
16) Corporate hoarding of residential property
17) Racial tension and conflict
18) Feminism & misogyny

We could go on for days. And the Jew has more legs than any octopus known to man. Each of the issues listed above represents a tentacle attached to the wicked head of the Jews. And since most of us don't know what a Jew is and how they work, we are panicking as we watch each of our proverbial ships being corralled and dragged under water to drown.

Thank goodness for the "Irritated Genie of Soufeese" (aka Ayo Kimathi): "People, I think I know what this is." You ask me, "Tell us what it is Genie. We're all going down." I say, "Jews Are The Problem." You ask me, "What's a Jew?" I say, "It's an evil hook-nosed creature working to exterminate most of the world's population and make those of us left behind into their slaves." You say, "What do we do?" I say, "Read this book. And after we decompress our minds from the magnitude of the threat we face due to the grip of their tentacles, the solution will easily present itself to us."

Any intelligent person should be able to finish this story. In my version, it has a happy ending.

Read this book with the seriousness that you had in the delivery room when your first child was born. It's truly a matter of life or death. And once you finish it, prepare yourself for an unavoidable clash with destiny. We will either wake up and do what is necessary, or we will all perish at the hands of the Jews.

JEWS ARE THE PROBLEM!

2

THE ULTIMATE GOALS AND PLAYBOOK OF THE JEWS

What does the Jew want? Simply stated, the Jew wants it all. They actually have a plan that is married onto their religious belief system that promises them the world. So, to understand them, we must take a cursory glance at both their religious beliefs and their political ideals. This combination will afford us a clear perspective on what the Jews actually want to accomplish.

Their religious beliefs are written down in their most holy of books called the Babylonian Talmud. This "holy" book of the Jews provides acceptance of rape, pedophilia, homosexuality, murder of non-Jews, theft from non-Jews, and promises the Jews they will one day rule over all of the people of the Earth. It also instructs Jews to never view non-Jews as people. All non-Jews are collectively viewed as Gentiles. We are also called *goyim* (singular: *goy*) or "sheep to be led to slaughter." In addition to being part of the *goyim*, Black people are called by the pejorative term *shvartza* in Jewish culture. It is the Jewish N-word.

The Babylonian Talmud is one of the most disgusting and perverse pieces of pornography I've ever come across. And the Jews pass this smut off as a religious text. No other "spiritual" text I am aware of endorses pedophilia of both boys and girls. This is Satanism and child pornography posing as a sacred Jewish religious text. Jeffrey Epstein would have been proud of his Jewish heritage if he were with us today. He lived his life in accordance with the laws of the Babylonian Talmud. The link to an article documenting Talmudic promotion of pedophilia is:

Pedophilia: The Talmud's Dirty Secret
goodnewsaboutgod.com/studies/political/jews/pedophilia.htm

In 2018, Sephardic Chief Rabbi of Israel Yitzhak Yosef referred to Black people, during a weekly sermon, using the derogatory term kushi, and referred to them as "monkeys"

The Talmud boldly endorses the murder of Gentiles. This is important to understand. Their religion is clear about them having authority to murder non-Jews. So, when they kill Palestinians, Syrians, Russians, or Black people in South Africa, they feel no empathy because it is part of their fundamental rights. And now that they are close to their final objective of world domination, the murder of the last strongholds of resistance against their agenda is currently underway. Our time is short. Their Babylonian Talmudic faith is centered in the belief in the day when Jews have successfully exterminated most of the world's population in order to become the "rightful rulers."

Europa **Part 5**
bitchute.com/video/TxCekvbTFzoa

The Jews are an incorrigible group of war merchants willing to push the planet to any conditions necessary to fulfill this result. They want any resistance to their total dominion removed from the planet at all costs. Nuclear war would be a small price to pay to achieve their objectives if it became necessary and/or desirable. Once their mission is completed, their belief is that those *goyim* remaining on the planet are here to be their submissive servants.

For a beneficial analysis and summary of what the Babylonian Talmud professes, we suggest you watch the video, *The Other Israel*:

The Other Israel
archive.org/details/theotherisraelhd

Their political agenda is captured in a book called *The Protocols of the Learned Elders of Zion*. This book was widely circulated to the American public by 1905. It's a literal roadmap of mass genocide on their way towards total world conquest. And the amazing thing about this book is that the Jews have followed this roadmap precisely to the letter with no regard for the fact that the plan is publicly available to purchase and distribute around the world. They universally deny the truth in the book while simultaneously executing the plan to a T.

Every tentacle of mass world destruction witnessed today is

outlined in the book. You name it—it's in there. And as of this moment, they've nearly completed their plans. They are a short distance from the mass genocide they desire and the enslavement of the remainder of the population.

Let's take a cursory glance at *aspects of some of the protocols* and see how they apply to the real-world situations we face today:

Protocol No. I

> **It must be remembered that people with base instincts are more numerous than those with noble ones; therefore, the best results in governing are achieved through violence and intimidation, and not through academic discussion.**

Both Presidents Abraham Lincoln and John F. Kennedy were murdered in cold blood. According to *The Synagogue of Satan* by Andrew Carrington Hitchcock, on page 66: "President Lincoln would be the last President to issue debt free United States notes." Lincoln stated, "We gave the people of this republic the greatest blessing they ever had, their own paper money to pay their own debts." These notes were called "Greenbacks" and Lincoln used them to finance the Union troops in the Civil War. He was killed on April 14, 1865 by a New York suspected Jew named John Wilkes Booth.

In a statement to Congress in 1865, President Lincoln said the following, "I have two great enemies, the Southern Army in the front of me, and the financial institutions in the rear. Of the two, the one in my rear is my greatest foe."

The Synagogue of Satan goes on to say on page 168: "On June 4, 1963, President John F. Kennedy (the 35th President of the United States 1961-1963) signs Executive Order 11110 which returns the United States Government the power to issue currency without going through the Rothschilds' owned Federal Reserve."

President Kennedy also made it perfectly clear he was not willing to budge one inch in allowing the nation of Israel to secure a nuclear weapon.

I offer these few historical facts as reference points for how the Jew operates. When anyone threatens their capacity to strangle society through financial dominance or attain desired weapons of mass destruction, they will bankrupt them, destroy their reputation, or kill them in the most violent and public means possible (if they are capable). Rulers of nations are no exception to this rule. They want everyone who matters to fear resisting their imperatives.

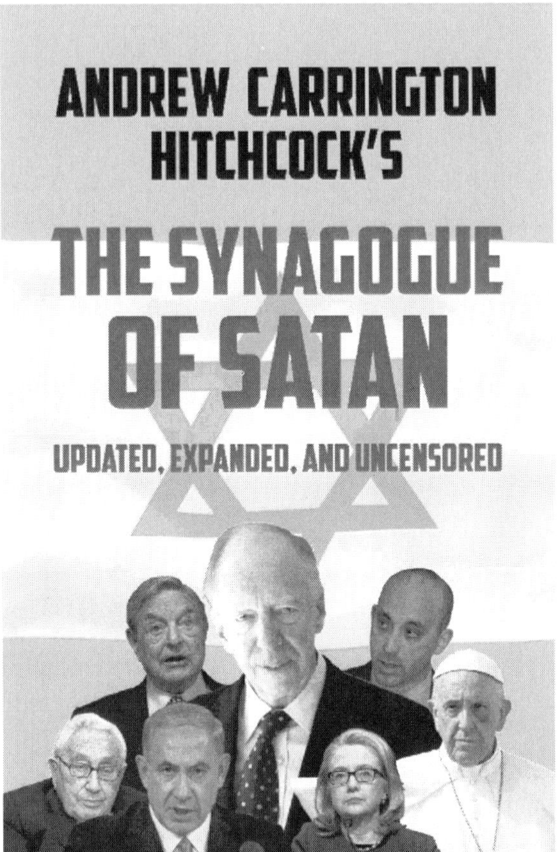

The Synagogue of Satan by Andrew Carrington Hitchcock
thesynagogueofsatan.com

Protocol No. II

Then our international rights will do away with national rights, in a limited sense, and will rule the peoples in the same way as the civil power of each state regulates the relation of its subjects among themselves.

This statement pefectly capsulizes the modern concept of Global Governance, One World Government, or New World Order (NWO). It speaks to the purpose of the United Nations (UN) and their "Global Agenda." Most people have at least heard of the NWO or the Global Agenda. What they haven't heard is that it is not simply a system of the "global elite." Rather, it is a system of powerful, organized Jews and their proxies.

The Jews are replacing sovereign nations with Jewish world hegemony where they are the single governing body of the Earth. When Donald Trump spoke at the UN, he declared open war against this agenda. He lost.

President Trump Declares the Future Belongs to Patriots
bitchute.com/video/YJGPHGyvHi6K

In 2022, the United States of America (U.S.) requested an amendment to the 2005 International Health Regulations (IHR). This is an international regulation that describes how the World Health Organization (WHO) and sovereign nations will interact with one another in the event of a major health crisis. The U.S. requested amendments that essentially remove sovereign nations from having a say in decisions about their countries and how they will identify and deal with health crises. The following is a very short snippet of one of the requested changes. The U.S. government requested the strikethrough line below to be removed:

Article 9: Other reports

> **1. WHO may take into account reports from sources other than notifications or consultations and shall assess these reports according to established epidemiological principles and then communicate information on the event to the State Party in whose territory the event is allegedly occurring. ~~Before taking any action based on such reports, WHO shall consult with and attempt to obtain verification from the State Party in whose territory the event is allegedly occurring in accordance with the procedure set forth in Article 10. To this end,~~ WHO shall make the information received available to the States Parties and only where it is duly justified may WHO maintain the confidentiality of the source. This information will be used in accordance with the procedure set forth in Article 11.**

As we can see here, the U.S. government wants to remove language that empowers countries to maintain sovereign authority over their nation's health crisis responses. Here, they refer to nations as "States Parties" and seek to put all of the power of each nation firmly into the hands of WHO. In short, if the amendment to IHR is accepted, WHO would have been granted the power to declare a pandemic in any region of the U.S. at its discretion, declare American citizens be rounded up and forcefully detained for a time period determined by them, mandate forced medical treatments and/or medications for Americans, and do so without any feedback from the U.S. government or its citizens. The U.S. Constitution would have been effectively rendered defunct. Largely due to the collective resistance by a unified group of Afrikan nations, this regulation was defeated, even though the desire and intention still exists.

In addition to this defeated amendment, WHO is working to create an international Treaty for Pandemic Prevention. If this "Treaty" is accepted by enough member nations, it will become legally binding for all the nations in WHO and will supersede the authority of the U.S. Constitution. This "Treaty" will strip nations of their sovereignty over their citizens' health decisions.

Protocol No. III

The aristocracy which benefited by the labor of the people by right was interested that the workers should be well fed, healthy, and strong.

We, on the contrary, are concerned in the opposite—in the degeneration of the GOYS. Our power lies in the chronic malnutrition and in the weakness of the worker, because through this he falls under our power and is unable to find either strength or energy to combat it.

Hunger gives to capital greater power over the worker than the legal authority of the sovereign ever gave to the aristocracy. Through misery and the resulting jealous hatred we manipulate the mob and crush those who stand in our way.

Jews have been architects of mass starvation pogroms and genocide throughout history. This is a major part of their world domination agenda.

Watch this *Europa* Part 1 link to get a visual perspective of how they've done it in the recent past in Eastern Europe:

Europa **Part 1**
bitchute.com/video/QtLvxZ9d0yEY

In today's America, they are orchestrating political unrest and national food shortages utilizing their positions in the Executive Branch of the U.S. government. As to not bore you with identifying each Jew responsible for every individual act of governmental abuse of the American people we discuss going forward, on a next page is a brief list of the positions they've held in the federal government under the Biden administration since Tuesday, March 16, 2022:

1) Doug Emhoff, husband of Vice President Kamala Harris
2) Janet Yellin, Secretary of Treasury
3) Anthony Blinken, Secretary of State
4) Robert Klain, Chief of Staff
5) David Cohen, Deputy Director CIA
6) Merrick Garland, Attorney General
7) Alejandro Mayorkas, Secretary Homeland Security
8) Avril Haines, Director National Intelligence
9) Wendy Sherman, Deputy Secretary of State
10) Victoria Nuland, Under Secretary of State for Political Affairs
11) Eric Lander, Director Office of Science and Technology Policy
12) Jeffrey Zients, Counselor to the President and COVID-19 Response Coordinator
13) Rachel Levine, Assistant Health Secretary
14) Cass Sunstein, Administrator Office of Information and Regulatory Affairs
15) Samantha Power, Administrator U.S. Agency for International Development (Sunstein's wife)
16) Dana Stroul, Deputy Assistant Secretary of Defense for the Middle East
17) Rochelle P. Walensky, Director Centers for Disease Control (CDC)
18) Anne Neuberger, Deputy National Security Advisor for Cybersecurity at NSA
19) Chanan Weissman, Director of Technology at National Security Council
20) Polly Trottenberg, Deputy Secretary of Transportation
21) Jessica Rosenworcel, Chairwoman Federal Communications Commission (FCC)
22) Jennifer Klein, Co-Chair of the Gender Policy Council
23) Jared Bernstein, Member of Council of Economic Advisers
24) David Kessler, Chief Science Officer of COVID Response & Head of Operation Warp Speed
25) Stephanie Pollack, Deputy Administrator Federal Highway Administration
26) Gary Gensler, Chairman of the Securities and Exchange Commission (SEC)
27) Mira Resnick, Deputy Assistant Secretary of Department of State
28) Roberta Jacobson, U.S. Ambassador to Mexico
29) Genine Macks Fidler, National Council on the Humanities
30) Deborah Lipstadt, Special Envoy to Monitor and Combat Anti-Semitism
31) Sharon Kleinbaum, Commissioner of U.S. Commission on International Religious Freedom

32) Jonathan Kanter, U.S. Assistant Attorney General Antitrust Division
33) Jed Kolko, Under Secretary of Commerce for Economic Affairs
34) Dan Shapiro, Advisor on Iran
35) Michele Taylor, U.S. Representative to UN Human Rights Council
36) Thomas Nides, U.S. Ambassador to Israel
37) Eric Garcetti, U.S. Ambassador to India
38) Amy Gutmann, U.S. Ambassador to Germany
39) David L. Cohen, U.S. Ambassador to Canada
40) Mark Gitenstein, U.S. Ambassador to European Union
41) Jonathan Kaplan, U.S. Ambassador to Singapore
42) Marc Stanley, U.S. Ambassador to Argentina
43) Rahm Emanuel, U.S. Ambassador to Japan
44) Alan Leventhal, U.S. Ambassador to Denmark
45) Michael Adler, U.S. Ambassador to Belgium
46) Stuart Eizenstat, Special Adviser on Holocaust Issues
47) Nina Jankowicz, Executive Director Disinformation Governance Board

Today, Jews *are* the executive branch of the American government!

Protocol No. IV

> **Who and what can overthrow an unseen power? For such is the character of our power.** ***External Masonry acts as a screen for it and its aims, but the plan of action of this power, and its very headquarters, will always remain unknown to the people.***

The fact American citizens are not up in arms about Biden's cabinet means most have no idea who and/or what we're dealing with. Consider, Jews make up about 2% of the U.S. population and over 50% of the Biden administration high positions. Shouldn't that be a concern for any American who doesn't want to be a Palestinian citizen of "Western Israel"?! Welcome my fellow Ameristinian (former American citizens now living under Biden's administration) readers, we're all in a pickle—and it's definitely a kosher one.

But the problem is the Jews look White to Black people and like a mirror to Anglo-Saxon Americans. Most people don't have a clue who they are, what they are, where they are, how to deal with them, or even why knowing anything about them is relevant. In other words, they're hiding from us in plain sight. They control our very lives and we don't even know they exist.

It is for this reason that we must undermine faith, tearing from the minds of the GOYS the very principle of God and Soul, and substituting mathematical formulas and material needs.

The attempt to destroy God by the Jew is an extension of their desire to become the gods of this Earth. Their designation of themselves as "God's Chosen People" is a reflection of the same desire to lord power over the people on this planet. And it is this very false identity and their belief in it that gives them the sense that they have the right to exterminate the Earth's population. They want the *goyim* to relinquish faith in an all-powerful creative force and turn instead to what they can see and prove. This reduces man from the spiritual to the physical level. Once we get stuck here, we lose hope and faith that we can defeat their evil designs.

Belief in the power of The Creator/God is a characteristic that has power beyond the natural world. It provides people with an illogical sense that they can defeat any force of evil or overcome any obstacle. It provides the spiritual fuel for miracles. Without this fuel, our current situation would appear completely hopeless to most people. This is what the Jews know and understand.

No video can express this any better than one by Dr. Yuval Noah Harari. He is a homophile transhumanist Jew, married to a man, who is the embodiment of the phrase, "We Shall Destroy God."

Dr. Yuval Noah Harari on Destroying God

bitchute.com/video/uOntnOE3vL8b

You heard it correctly. This group actually intends to take over the creation process and start making their own species of beings while destroying the natural order. If we are not careful, we will actually allow them to genetically implant wombs in the DNA of males before they are born. This would be the kind of world Harari would like to live in; and now they have the technology to produce it.

Protocol No. V

> **Temporarily, a world coalition of the GOYS would be able to hold us in check, but we are insured against this by roots of dissension so deep among them that they cannot now be extracted. We have set at variance the personal and national interests of the GOYS; we have incited religious and race hatred, nurtured by us in their hearts for twenty centuries. Owing to all this, no state will obtain the help it asks for from any side because each of them will think that a coalition against us will be disadvantageous to it. We are too powerful—we must be taken into consideration. No country can reach even an insignificant private understanding without our being secret parties to it.**

This is so relevant in today's environment. Donald Trump won the 2020 election, but is not in office. A powerful group of Black activists knew his loss would be disastrous and result in a similar fate to the country as we are witnessing today. In August 2020, we met with the White House to secure resources for the Black community in exchange for a plan of action that would have guaranteed Trump the victory and made it very hard to take it away from him. The White House loved the proposal; however, we could not get a meeting with President Trump himself. Our plan made it all the way to Jared Kushner, but he did not afford the team an opportunity to meet with President Trump who would have *loved* the proposal.

Had President Trump had an Anglo-Saxon who was more strategic than emotional as his point man, we would have gotten the meeting and he would still be in office. Things would have still been difficult for Black people, and police misconduct (domestic terrorism against Black people) would have risen. But we would have received significant benefits and not been facing the collapse of the economy, forced injection mandates, rising unemployment, hiked gas prices, food shortages, pedophile-friendly Supreme Court justice nominations, and the potential for a traditional-styled WWIII.

Jews make sure aggressive, self-respecting Black leadership and powerful Anglo-Saxons never sit down at the negotiating table without them present. It is a traumatizing fear of theirs. They know the most dangerous combination of forces against their tyranny are Black Nationalists and Anglo-Saxons. These are the two most violent and capable groups when they organize to resist opposition forces.

And even if the Jew was not there to stop the meeting, it is difficult for Black people to meet and work with rich, conservative Anglo-Saxons. Both groups have a hostility toward one another that has been developed over centuries of life in America. And as we proceed in this book, we will see that much of the animosity was instigated by Jews. It has been their best weapon at managing the overthrow of this Republic—pitting Anglo-Saxons and Black people against one another.

The current situation with Russia, Ukraine, NATO, and the U.S. is a pivotal moment in history. As of March 20, 2022, we do not know how far this war will go. What we do know is Black Americans have 1000X more in common with Russia than Ukraine. We do not like homophilia, fighting in unnecessary wars, being slandered by the media, crossdressing Jewish leaders (Zelenskyy in Ukraine), NWO ordinances and agendas, famine, hyperinflation, chemical/biological warfare (we remember Tuskegee), cannibals, Ukrainian racists (would not allow Afrikan people to flee the country), child sex-trafficking, illegal organ harvesting, slavery, etc. Russia openly expresses disdain for these practices. Ukraine is known for engaging in these behaviors. Black people are not aligned with Ukraine on any level.

This could be a basis for dialog between Black people worldwide and the Russian government. If we share similar values and agree that many of these issues are major concerns to civilization, we should at least discuss this diplomatically.

President Volodymyr Zelenskyy of Ukraine—Gay Music Video
bitchute.com/video/K8ihk5FbWhGY

President Vladimir Putin in younger days w/Afrikan liberation leaders

In the U.S., anyone paying attention can plainly see it was the Jews who overthrew the American Republic with Barack Hussein Obama and overthrew it again with the stolen election of Joe Biden. Accordingly, different people around the world have lots to discuss.

But let us remember the Protocol above. In part it says, **"Owing to all this, no state will obtain the help it asks for from any side because each of them will think that a coalition against us will be disadvantageous to it."** If the Jews are correct, this means Russia is not free enough, even while fighting genetic annihilation at the hands of the same group, to openly and publicly expose and discuss the source of the problem. Even the mighty Russian Bear has to be very careful when addressing their Jew problem.

I will discuss the solution to this very real problem later in the book.

To control public opinion it is necessary to perplex it by the expression of numerous contradictory opinions until the GOYS get lost in the labyrinth, and come to understand that it is best to have no opinion on political questions.

Such questions are not intended to be understood by the people, since only he who rules knows them. This is the first secret.

Transgenderism, Critical Race Theory (CRT), LGBT, anti-vaxxers, sex education in schools, non-binary, "gender fluidity," the "New Normal," the "New Family," "gender neutrality," "race neutrality," tolerance, homophobic, transphobic, heteronormative, liberalism, conservatism, communism, Marxism, socialism, capitalism, "minor-attracted," Putin the Monster, Trump the Monster, Dr. Khalid Abdul Muhammad the Monster, Irritated Genie of Soufeese the Monster, feminism, "toxic masculinity," Biden "Crack Pipes for Good Health," "post racial," New World Order, One World Government, misogyny, "Woke" culture, etc.

Many of us are at least generally familiar with these themes and concepts. Many of them we do not exactly understand. Others we do not like and/or agree with. Nevertheless, these are among the rubric of concepts and ideas spreading throughout America and the world. At a point, they become so many and so bizarre, that we throw our hands in the air in frustration and stop thinking about any of it.

This exhaustion is exactly what the Jews look for as their cue to intensify their propaganda war to the next phase.

Protocol No. VI

The aristocracy of the GOYS as a political force is dead. We do not need to take it into consideration; but as landowners they are harmful to us because they can be independent in their resources of life. For this reason we must deprive them of their land at any cost.

More than anything else, the Jew is an enslaver. Like a parasite enslaves the health of its host(s) by feeding off its blood without the host being aware, the Jew always seeks to weaken its host by sucking the mental, moral, and economic lifeblood out of it for Jewish sustenance.

The history of Europe is of Whites struggling to survive the parasitic invasion and overthrow of their communities, regions, or nations by subversive money-grabbing Jews. The history is 100% clear and has been well-documented. This Jewish seizure of the wealth and resources of Europeans reads like a bad episode of *Pinky and the Brain*. Go! Some White country is doing relatively well. The Jews, Ashkenazim or Sephardim, find a way to get in. They become merchants. They create debt. They become rich while the people become poor. They begin to sex-traffic women and children. They popularize some form of pornography. They turn the country into a blazing immoral inferno of filth and indecency. Some prophet figures out who did it and how. They go to the people to identify the Jew as the problem. The people all compare their debts, losses, and foreclosures and realize they've been had. Then either of two things happen:

1) The Jews kill the prophet and the people become outraged.

2) The people organize to get the Jews out of town.

No matter which of these occurs, the Jews ostentatiously display their arrogance and egotism and use whatever power they have to repel the people's will. When this doesn't work, the people start directly attacking Jews physically and reclaim their land and resources. The Jews who aren't killed in the melee of the people's resentment, flee town for their lives in the face of certain death. Lastly, the surviving Jews move to another unsuspecting host group and complain how horribly they were oppressed and mistreated for being Jews. The people let them in and . . . rewind. Start at Go!

Jews and the African Slave Trade

Throughout the history of the practice, Jews have been involved in the purchase and sale of human beings. This fact is confirmed by their own scholars and historians. In his book *A History of the Jews*, Solomon Grayzel states that "Jews were among the most important slave dealers" in European society.[3] Lady Magnus writes that in the Middle Ages, "The principal purchasers of slaves were found among the Jews....[T]hey seemed to be always and everywhere at hand to buy, and to have the means equally ready to pay."[4] Henry L. Feingold stated that "Jews who were frequently found at the heart of commerce could not have failed to contribute a proportionate share to the [slave] trade directly or indirectly. In 1460, when Jews were the masters of the nautical sciences in Portugal, that nation was importing 700-800 slaves yearly."[5]

The success of these medieval merchants was enhanced by their supreme linguistic abilities. They spoke Arabic, Persian, Roman, Frankish, Spanish and Slavonic and "displayed a business acumen far in advance of the times."[6]

The Secret Relationship Between Blacks and Jews Volume 1 by Nation of Islam (NOI) Research Department (p. 9)

10 The Secret Relationship Between Blacks and Jews

The Jews' participation in the slave trade, particularly their trafficking in non-Jewish slaves, incited the moral indignation of Europe's Gentile population. The Europeans reacted by taxing the Jews and some were expelled from their host countries for this activity.[7] The expulsion of Jews by European governments was not unusual, with most of the complaints centered around economic exploitation, monopolizing, or "sharp practice." By 1500, with the exception of certain parts of Italy, Western Europe had closed its doors to Jewish people.[8] The following listing is a partial record of the countries and dates of the Jews' expulsion from various European communities.[9]

Mainz, 1012
France, 1182
Upper Bavaria, 1276
England, 1290
France, 1306
France, 1322
Saxony, 1349
Hungary, 1360
Belgium, 1370
Slovakia, 1380
France, 1394
Austria, 1420
Lyons, 1420
Cologne, 1424
Mainz, 1438
Augsburg, 1439
Upper Bavaria, 1442
Netherlands, 1444
Brandenburg, 1446
Mainz, 1462
Mainz, 1483
Warsaw, 1483
Spain, 1492
Italy, 1492
Lithuania, 1495
Portugal, 1496
Naples, 1496
Navarre, 1498
Nuremberg, 1498
Brandenburg, 1510
Prussia, 1510
Genoa, 1515
Naples, 1533
Italy, 1540
Naples, 1541
Prague, 1541
Genoa, 1550
Bavaria, 1551
Prague, 1557
Papal States, 1569
Hungary, 1582
Hamburg, 1649
Vienna, 1669
Slovakia, 1744
Bohemia/Moravia, 1744
Moscow, 1891

Over the next centuries the centers of Jewish development moved into the Western Hemisphere, where land and commercial opportunities provided the incentives for immigration. The open and ungoverned territory and the docile and vulnerable indigenous population were an irresistible attraction to the "maligned race." They acquired great wealth in their Caribbean

Jews and the African Slave Trade 11

and South American enterprises and eventually moved into the American Northeast, which became the economic focal point. It started with the forced expulsion of the Jews from the Spanish empire and with the early explorer and "discoverer" of America, Christopher Columbus.

The Secret Relationship Between Blacks and Jews Volume 1 by Nation of Islam (NOI) Research Department (pp. 10-11)

The Secret Relationship Between Blacks and Jews Vol 1
socialarchitects26.com/The-Secret-Relationship-Between-Blacks-&-Jews-1-$20-p454422058

The pages of this classic piece of literature shown above give a glimpse into the historical addiction of the Jew for enslaving.

Protocol No. VIII

We must provide ourselves with the same arms our enemies can employ against us. We must seek the most subtle expressions and evasions of the legal dictionary to justify those cases in which we will be forced to announce decisions which may seem unnecessarily bold and unjust, for it is important that these decisions should be expressed in terms so forceable that they will appear as the highest moral rules of a legal character.

> Our government must be surrounded by all the forces of civilization, in the midst of which it will have to function. It will surround itself with publicists, experienced lawyers, administrators, diplomats, and, finally, people educated along special lines in our special advanced schools.
>
> These people will know all the secrets of social existence; they will know all languages composed of political letters and words; they will be familiar with the reverse side of human nature, with all its sensitive chords, upon which they must know how to play. These chords are the structure of mind of the intellects of the GOYS, their tendencies, their failings, their vices, and their virtues, the peculiarities of classes and castes. It is evident that the highly talented members of our government, to which I refer, will be recruited not from the ranks of the GOYS, accustomed to performing their administrative duties without questioning their aim, and without thinking why they are necessary. The GOY administrators sign papers without reading them and work for profit or for pride.

This point in Protocol No. VIII can be summed up by two current issues in the news:

NATO & World Economic Forum (WEF)

As it relates to weapons, NATO is the primary tool for the Jews to arm themselves and their proxies with military weapons (e.g., Ukraine).

NATO Countries Providing Weapons to Ukraine
aljazeera.com/news/2022/2/28/which-countries-are-sending-military-aid-to-ukraine

WEF is the prototype for training the *goyim* in the agenda of global Jewish hegemony. This organization, founded by Klaus

Schwab (trained by Jews Henry Kissinger and Herman Kahn), has organized young non-Jews of all races and young Jews from around the world in preparation for this Jewish world overthrow. These young *"goyim"* leaders are part of groups called "Global Leaders for Tomorrow," and "Young Global Leaders." These two groups are the epitome of elite proxy groups educated and trained to implement and fulfill the global conquest agenda of the Jews.

The WEF and the Pandemic
swprs.org/the-wef-and-the-pandemic

Young Global Leaders
younggloballeaders.org

The primary difference between these groups and everyday people who are supporting this agenda is that they have been informed. They are not blindly and unknowingly supporting the program. They have been given the insight of the Jews and the purpose for the decisions being made. They are all willing and knowing participants in the genocide of the planet on behalf of Jewish hegemony.

Protocol No. IX

We have misled, corrupted, fooled, and demoralized the youth of the Goys by education along principles and theories known by us to be false but which we ourselves have inspired.

The Jews control Western education and media. This is something most people are clear on. For those who are not, here is a brief insight into who owns most of the Western mainstream media (MSM) and social media platforms.

[Author's note: Media moguls buy and sell networks on a regular basis, so the particulars change all the time. But this gives a snapshot of who owns the world's primary media outlets at any given moment.]

Google & YouTube's Larry Page and Sergey Brin

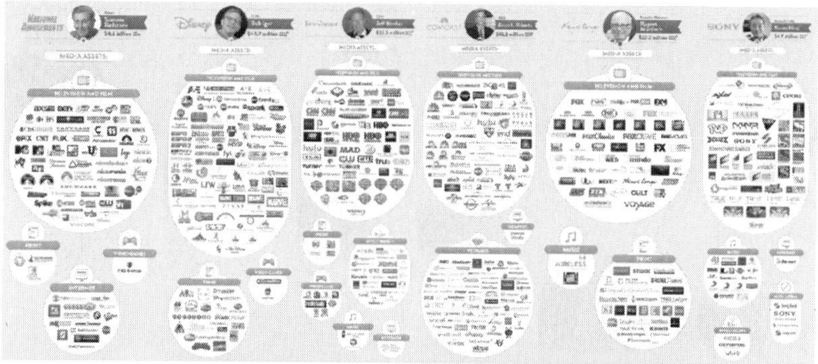

Facebook's Mark Zuckerberg

Through media of all sorts, Jews have intentionally destroyed the minds of American youth on a level difficult to quantify. Pedophilia, homosexuality, Satanism, crossdressing, drug abuse, promiscuity, crime and violence, laziness, disrespect, dishonesty, theft, immorality, stupidity and ignorance, poor health habits, public nudity, materialism, irresponsibility, etc. are common themes taught to children in schools, cartoons, television programs, movies, modern churches, music, and throughout the society. Our youth have been holistically put under siege by a destructive culture determined to under develop their thinking and behavior.

Fairfax County, VA Mother Fights Schoolboard Over Pedophilia in School Books—Jewish Board Member Interrupts Mother
bitchute.com/video/TlaxiwEmoukk

Protocol No. X

> **. . . it is necessary continuously to disturb the relationship between the people and the government in all countries, and so to exhaust everybody by the dissension, hostility, struggle, hatred, and even martyrdom, hunger, inoculation of diseases, and misery, and to make the Goys see no other solution than an appeal to our money and complete rule.**
>
> *Should we give the people a rest, however, the longed for moment will probably never arrive.* [Emphasis added]

This is almost a precise description of the COVID-19 "pandemic." For the rest of this book, we will often refer to anything related to COVID-19 as "The Fauci." What we called COVID-19 (The Fauci) is actually *WWIII*. We are waiting for the traditional warfare between NATO and Russia to let us know the war has begun. We don't realize the Pearl Harbor of WWIII was the release of the U.S.-funded gain-of-function research (GoFR) bioweapon, The Fauci. This agent of destruction was tailored and released in order to launch an international war against the world's population. In this war, there are no civilians!

The release of this weapon was designed to send panic throughout the planet. The purpose was to scare people into willingly accepting the more dangerous bioweapon dishonestly classified as the "vaccination." In order to do this, they implemented procedures at hospitals throughout the U.S. to kill as many as possible—Black and Anglo-Saxon. To this day, they have a procedural guideline that makes hospitals rich through a process of killing patients.

Since the 2021 release of the harmful injections called "vaccines," hospitals are paid for everyone they give a polymerase chain reaction (PCR) test. They are paid again for every positive PCR test. If they admit the patient for care, they receive another payment. After admission, the only authorized drug to administer is remdesivir, a drug known to kill people and that has 0% effectiveness in protecting against The Fauci. Hospitals receive a 20% incentive fee to prescribe this poison to patients. When remdesivir destroys their kidneys, they can no longer pass liquid through them. Therefore, the liquid from their kidneys backs up into their lungs and makes it difficult to breath. Then the medical staff sticks a ventilator into or down their throats and collects a whopping $39,000 payment. By the time the process ends, they can make as much as $100,000 on one patient. The last payment is made if the death certificate says COVID-19 (The Fauci).

Dr. Peterson Pierre Explains the Process for Murder by Remdesivir

bitchute.com/video/KQ8XpSsfbxVC

I described this process to show the parallels with Protocol No. X. This is a clear process of struggle, inoculation of diseases, torture, and murder. The Jews enrich themselves at the life expense of others. How so you might ask?

Not only are many of the owners of the hospitals and doctors and nurses Jewish, but Jews also control the pharmaceutical companies. Some of the Jewish contributors to this international plandemic genocide are as follows:

COVID-19 Pharmaceutical Control

If this is not enough, these harmful injections are not vaccinations. They are dangerous technology designed to destroy our natural immune systems, rewrite our DNA codes, insert Artificial Intelligence (AI) into our bodies for control, and kill us. Any leaders who make an effort to resist this global injection genocide are removed from power or killed. Former President Bolsonaro of Brazil was robbed of reelection in November 2022 partly due to his firm anti-injection stance. This election theft, mirroring the 2020 Trump stolen election, may lead to significant unrest and violence in Brazil.

In the process of implementing this DNA-altering technology, they have managed to turn peoples of almost all nations against their corrupt governments. The Jews trained and paid disruptive rioters and rebel rousers to instigate unrest in America and other countries around the world in the same fashion they orchestrated the overthrow of Ukraine in 2014. Victoria Nuland, Jew of Ukrainian descent and Biden executive branch appointee, was heavily involved in orchestrating the overthrow and replacement of the duly elected Ukrainian president in 2014.

The Jews systematically orchestrated the theft of the 2020 U.S. presidential election to push their plans forward without resistance. To view detailed proof of the fact that the Jews stole the 2020 election, order this video set:

Smallhats: Mortal Enemies to Planet Earth **(3-DVD Set)**
Including Disc 2: "Who Stole the 2020 Election?"
Electronic Email Download MP4 Version
socialarchitects26.com/Smallhats-Mortal-Enemy-to-Planet-Earth-3-Disc-DVD-Set-mp4-Electronic-Email-Version-p279862011

Hard Copy through USPS Mail

socialarchitects26.com/Smallhats-Mortal-Enemy-to-Planet-Earth-3-Disc-DVD-Set-p279854032

After they had full control of the White House again (first time was under Obama), they immediately rolled out the bioweapon injection war against the people of the world. Once people took the shots, the numbers of injuries and deaths skyrocketed. To this very day, these injections have proven more dangerous and harmful than any medication in U.S. history. These are international figures from WHO as of January 15, 2023:

vigiaccess.org

VigiAccess World Health Organization

COVID-19 vaccine is an active ingredient
There are **4 846 059** reports with this active ingredient

Reported potential side effects

- Blood and lymphatic system disorders (2%, 208 101 ADRs)
- Cardiac disorders (3%, 289 690 ADRs)
- Congenital, familial and genetic disorders (0%, 3 444 ADRs)
- Ear and labyrinth disorders (1%, 138 573 ADRs)
- Endocrine disorders (0%, 10 708 ADRs)
- Eye disorders (1%, 155 441 ADRs)
- Gastrointestinal disorders (7%, 812 205 ADRs)
- General disorders and administration site conditions (26%, 2 914 974 ADRs)
- Hepatobiliary disorders (0%, 10 955 ADRs)
- Immune system disorders (1%, 84 867 ADRs)
- Infections and infestations (5%, 589 790 ADRs)
- Injury, poisoning and procedural complications (3%, 297 225 ADRs)
- Investigations (7%, 740 862 ADRs)
- Metabolism and nutrition disorders (1%, 91 322 ADRs)
- Musculoskeletal and connective tissue disorders (10%, 1 183 619 ADRs)
- Neoplasms benign, malignant and unspecified (incl cysts and polyps) (0%, 12 162 ADRs)
- Nervous system disorders (16%, 1 796 330 ADRs)
- Pregnancy, puerperium and perinatal conditions (0%, 12 955 ADRs)
- Product issues (0%, 9 879 ADRs)
- Psychiatric disorders (2%, 225 892 ADRs)
- Renal and urinary disorders (0%, 40 996 ADRs)
- Reproductive system and breast disorders (2%, 256 480 ADRs)
- Respiratory, thoracic and mediastinal disorders (4%, 488 509 ADRs)
- Skin and subcutaneous tissue disorders (5%, 554 949 ADRs)
- Social circumstances (0%, 41 557 ADRs)
- Surgical and medical procedures (1%, 104 717 ADRs)
- Vascular disorders (2%, 221 531 ADRs)

If we add to this international crisis by including the mask mandates, insurance policies not honored due to taking the harmful injection, lack of socializing, pending food shortages, soaring gas prices, etc., we see that we are being slow cooked and tortured just as *The Protocols* expressed over 120 years ago:

> *When we accomplish our coup d'état, we will say to the peoples: "Everything went badly; all of you have suffered. We will abolish the cause of your sufferings, that is to say, nationalities, frontiers, and national currencies. Of course you are free to condemn us, but would your judgment be just if you were to pronounce it before giving a trial to what we will give you?" Thereafter they will exalt us with a sentiment of unanimous delight and hope. The voting*

system which we have used as a tool for our enthronement, and to which we have accustomed even the most humble members of humanity by organizing meetings and prearranged agreements, will have performed its last service and will make its last appearance in the expression of a unanimous desire to become more closely acquainted with us before having pronounced a judgment.

The Jews know some people will discover what they are doing before they complete their agenda. So, in the interest of being steps ahead of the masses, they have introduced the world to the concept called "The Great Reset" through Klaus Schwab, the founder of the WEF mentioned above. This idea is gaining greater exposure in society. Schwab forecasts that by the year 2030 a new world government will exist that has globally eliminated national sovereignty. By 2030, he says, all individual freedoms and rights will be turned over to the new international world government and personal property rights including land ownership will no longer exist. One of his infamous quotes associated with The Great Reset is that by the year 2030, "You will own nothing and be happy." He reasons everyone will be satisfied living in a state of techno-slavery where people are one with robots and are satisfied with accepting whatever rations the One World Government authorizes them to have. Schwab also forecasts America will no longer be the world's superpower by 2030.

We would be a bit less disturbed if these were predictions being made by someone foreseeing the future. In this case, these are not predictions. These are targeted goals which Jews and their proxies are actively working to achieve.

Lastly, Schwab has made it perfectly clear that he is on board with the use of AI in order to merge the human genome with computer technology. This is a process called "transhumanism."

In short, Schwab is managing the Jewish hegemony transition process where the world will be bankrupted, starved, poisoned, warred, sex-trafficked, and killed in such a beleaguering manner that we will peacefully surrender to their absolute dominion. Or so they think?

WEF—The Great Reset Page
weforum.org/agenda/2020/07/klaus-schwab-nature-jobs-great-reset-podcast

Klaus Schwab's Eight Forecasts for 2030
medium.com/illumination/in-2030-youll-own-nothing-and-be-happy-about-it-abb2835bd3d1

Jews Are The Problem is an indication that the Jews and their proxies are in for a rude awakening. We will not go peacefully. We will not go.

Protocol No. XI

> **The GOYS are like a flock of sheep—we are wolves. Do you know what happens to sheep when wolves get into the fold?**

Two shining examples of the Zionist wolves eating their proverbial *goyim* prey are, 1) the election of Obama, and, 2) the Russia/Ukraine war.

In 2008, the Jews took an irrelevant, unknown mulatto homophile politician out of Illinois and made him the president of the United States of America. He had no *publicly known* relevant legislation in his resume. He had no major political achievements. He had a Black "wife" and two children—and that's about all he appeared to have been doing correctly.

The Jews were so bold and callous about this move, that they steamrolled one of the most dangerous Anglo-Saxon political families in America—the Clintons. They never once got concerned about being a part of the infamous Clinton body count. After all, **"Who and what can overthrow an unseen power?"** (Protocol No. IV)

Clinton Body Count Documentary
bitchute.com/video/4I81nVNND8uM

The 2008 election of Obama as president was a clear example of the U.S. public being led like a pack of sheep into the wolves' den for dinner. Both Black people and Anglo-Saxons piled in lines waiting to vote for a warmongering Jewish front man who would go on to launch wars in North Afrika, assassinate sovereign leaders like Muammar Gaddafi, promote homophilia around the planet like a gay pied piper, push the federal government to legalize gay marriage, ignore the domestic terrorism and murder of innocent Black people in America by the police, ignore murderers of Black children like George Zimmerman who wears a very Jewish name, etc. He ignored *every* major issue dear to Black people and never stopped utilizing the power of his position to push the LGBT agenda.

Ironically, in 2005 U.S. Senator Barack Obama co-brokered the deal for the U.S. to start funding the bioweapons laboratories in Ukraine. So, in many ways, he is directly involved in creating the bioweapon crisis we see in the world today. Yet, this is the man who drew tears from American citizens as they sheepishly fumbled en masse to an imaginary space of post-racial euphoria that never existed. As a result of this naivety, we paid for our own moral, social, political, and racial destruction.

Barack Obama Co-brokers Deal to Fund Bioweapon Labs in Ukraine in 2005
washingtonpost.com/archive/politics/2005/08/30/us-to-aid-ukraine-in-countering-bioweapons/72059ed1-90ca-4381-ac6f-10f4e205f09e

Ariyana Love on Stew Peters
rumble.com/vxp4eh-horrifying-russian-report-ukrainian-biolabs-creating-special-bioweapons-for.html

Everybody is being destroyed by the trick of Obama except two groups: Jews and homophiles. These two groups are actually one group. Jews control the entire LGBT movement. They created and funded it from its inception.

Brother Nathanael on the Plot to Make America Gay
brothernathanaelchannel.com/watch_video.php?v=1076

The magic in the election of Obama is that it was impossible to occur by natural means in 2008. Only through the power of the Jewish media and political influence was such a horrible idea made into a reality. And they got the masses on board with our own destruction.

The second blatant example of the sheep being led to slaughter is the U.S. position in the Russia/Ukraine war. Many Black and Anglo-Saxon citizens are on board with funding Ukraine with billions of U.S. dollars' worth of military equipment for the war against Russia. Some U.S. citizens, Anglo-Saxon and Black, are volunteering their services to fight on the ground against the trained Russian forces. Many American citizens are even calling for the U.S. to "nuke" Russia and do harm to President Putin.

For Black people to support Ukraine in this war is utterly

preposterous. Ukraine blocked our Afrikan Brothers and Sisters from fleeing the country when the war began. They have also approached Black civilians and pressured them to join the war. Luckily, many have resisted. Nevertheless, this is a blatantly racist and hostile country to Black people and there is no reason for us to support it.

For Anglo-Saxons in America to support Ukraine in this war is complete and utter suicidal genocide. They are not thinking at all. The Jews have opened their southern borders to let foreigners load in by the hundreds of thousands. They've imported over 100,000 people from Middle Eastern countries the U.S. bombed over the past 20 years. They're promoting interracial marriage through the media as if same-race marriage is a crime. Homophilia is spreading through this country like soft butter and it is aimed at our young generations who are in their reproductive season. Whites are not producing enough children to replenish their numbers and Anglo-Saxons everywhere are talking about their racial survival. Yet, at the very same time, the Jews have American Anglo-Saxons preparing to load up and travel thousands of miles across seas to murder the last surviving powerful White nation on the planet. Russians will defend themselves and kill back. And all the White folks with guns will murder each other and leave Israel standing as the world power, with China as its underling.

While this is occurring, the Jews are publicly lecturing on the complete extermination of the Anglo-Saxon.

Rabbi Lectures to Arabs to Extirpate Amalek
(Exterminate the White Race)
bitchute.com/video/JdW3Bb6NJzJM

As a Black man, watching this play out is amazing. I actually get to see the Jews inspire Anglo-Saxons to get excited about murdering their Russian brothers and sisters with the same zeal Jews get them to want to kill Black people. Watching MSM is like watching a Jewish-sponsored Ku Klux Klan (KKK) pep rally against Russia. If my own people weren't doing the exact same thing right now, I'd be calling you the stupidest group of people on the planet. However, whenever the Western Israeli Jews control the narrative, all Ameristinians are equal idiots.

Cameroonian Refuses to Fight for Ukraine
bitchute.com/video/rdPUX9ofPRhv

American Volunteer Fleeing Ukraine
bitchute.com/video/KANulEggiZlT

They will also close their eyes to everything because we will promise to return to them all their liberties after the enemies of peace have been subjugated and all the parties pacified.

Is it necessary to say how long they would have to wait for the return of their liberties?

The Fauci. Two weeks, two months, next year, Jab 1, Jab 2, Booster, Booster for Booster, masks on children, electronic digital passports, slavery, genocide, New Normal, long COVID, etc.

Life is never going back to the way it was before The Fauci. We will either subdue the Jew or we will all perish.

Why have we conceived and inspired this policy for the GOYS without giving them an opportunity to examine its inner meaning if not for the purpose of attaining by a circuitous method what is unattainable for our scattered race by a direct road?

> **This constituted a base for our organization of** *secret masonry which is not known to and whose aims are not even suspected by these cattle, the Goys. They have been decoyed by us into our numerous ostensible organizations, which appear to be Masonic lodges, so as to divert the attention of their coreligionists.*

The plan is the global extermination of the world's population with a few *goyim* left behind to act as slaves to the Jews. The illusion of inclusion into high society for the *goyim* are the Masonic lodges, Masonic temples, secret societies, religious orders, money elite clubs, etc.

This is easy to see in today's society. Masons of all races secretly plan and organize. However, nothing they have learned is having any impact on the overthrow of the American Republic. And if they so much as tried to use their Masonic influence to challenge the agenda, even at a 33° level, they will be summarily executed in cold blood. If they actually had real power, the Masons would have avoided the injection war. To my knowledge, they did not.

Where this influence is best seen publicly is in the entertainment industry. For quite a few pieces of silver and a few bars of gold, entertainers in the West sell their very souls to the Jews. They travel the Earth consistently making symbolic hand gestures to show their allegiance to the "Illuminati." They believe they are part of something great because after they bend back up off of the couch, they are filthy rich. *Filthy. Rich.* But they do not actually belong to anything other than the system of their own genocide. They are no more a part of the Illuminati than a field slave is part of the cotton plantation. And as some of them have found out, running away from the industry can sometimes be as deadly as fleeing the slave plantation.

active beauty

Tom Cruise
Ben Stiller
Al Sharpton
Warren Buffett
Denzel Washington
Christina Agulera
Drake
Victor Cruz
Kanye West
James Lebron
Rihanna
Beyoncé

To be clear, I am in no way insinuating that each of these people in the pictures above believe themselves to be part of some type of secret order. Many of them may be innocently posing for pictures using popular poses. But for certain, some of them are doing it as part of some type of bizarre cultish association with Jews who pay them millions of dollars in exchange for their souls. This is real and it is uncomfortable.

Most importantly, they are part of nothing other than their own enslavement and the genocide of their respective races.

> **God has given us, his chosen people, the power to scatter, and what to all appears to be our weakness, has proved to be our strength, and has now brought us to the threshold of universal rule.**

Here, the Jews demonstrate their sense of group loyalty by defining themselves as being beyond any national or international boundaries. They are Jews more than anything. And they somehow cleverly took their misfortune at having been run out of almost every region of the planet they have temporarily inhabited as a gift from God. It has afforded them the opportunity to be parasites in any region of the Earth they deem suitable for their world subjugation conquest agenda. And no matter in what country they reside, they are still Jews.

Jews are now seeing their world conquest vision within a few clicks of landing on shore. They are almost there.

Jews Are The Problem brings us to the reckoning with the Jews at the crossroads of survival.

Protocol No. XII

> **Liberty is the right to do that which is permitted by law. Such a definition of this word will eventually serve us, because liberty will be in our power; and also because the laws will either destroy or construct only what we desire in accordance with the above mentioned program.**

The U.S. Constitution has been cleverly replaced by a new book. Just as the Jews have used their power in Congress, law, and education to replace the American belief in and adherence to the Holy Bible with adopting the principles of the Babylonian Talmud, so have they done with the U.S. Constitution. The U.S. Constitution has been quietly replaced by *The Protocols of the Learned Elders of Zion*. As a result, we see bills targeting our Constitutional First Amendment (Amendment 1) right to free speech, under the guise of targeting "anti-Semitism," popping up all over the country. This is why we refer to America under this current rule as Western Israel. In this country today, Jews are THE LAW.

For a detailed explanation of the Jewish overthrow of the U.S. Constitution and traditional American values, order the 3-DVD set below:

Hard Copy through USPS Mail
socialarchitects26.com/Smallhats-Mortal-Enemy-to-Planet-Earth-3-Disc-DVD-Set-p279854032

Not one notice will be made public without our control. This is already being done by us, since the news from all parts of the world is received through several agencies in which it is centralized.

These agencies will then be completely in our power and they will publish only such news as we will permit.

The Jewish control of media has already been established. This grilling of the Jews who control social media in Congress is a recent example of this reality:

U.S. Senator Josh Hawley (R-MO) in Senate Judiciary Hearing w/Big Tech
bitchute.com/video/B-5IwpAz0sU

Protocol No. XV

The GOYS become members of the lodges out of pure curiosity, or hoping to receive their share in the public funds. There are others who come for the purpose of seizing the opportunity of putting before the public their impossible and baseless hopes. They long for the emotion of success and for the applause which we grant them lavishly. We create their success in order to utilize the self-deception that is born with it and by which people, without noticing, begin to follow our suggestions without suspecting them, and being fully convinced that their infallibility

> originates its own ideas and, therefore, does not need those of others. You have no idea how easy it is to bring even the most intelligent GOYS to a state of unconscious credulity, and, on the other hand, how easy it is to discourage them by the smallest failure, or merely by ceasing to applaud them, thus bringing them into servitude for the sake of achieving new success. *To the same extent as our people ignore success for the sake of carrying out their plans, so are the GOYS ready to sacrifice all their plans for the sake of success.* Their psychology makes the problem of direction easier for us. Those tigers in appearance have the souls of sheep and nonsense filters through their heads. As a hobby we have given them the dream of submerging human individualism through the symbolic idea of *collectivism.*
>
> They have not yet discovered and will not discover that this hobby is a clear infringement on the principal law of nature, which, from the beginning of the world, created a being unlike all others, precisely for the sake of expressing his individuality.
>
> If we were able to lead them to such insane and blind beliefs, does it not obviously prove the low level of development of the GOY mind as compared to our mind? It is precisely the thing which guarantees our success.

This is self-explanatory. When Whoopi Goldberg said the killing of Jews in Nazi Germany was not about race, but rather it was a fight between two ethnic groups, she was fundamentally correct. She pretended like she was going to hold her ground. However, when her handlers suspended her from *The View*, she bowed down before her masters and remembered who was in charge.

Whoopi Goldberg Suspended from *The View*
bitchute.com/video/PUvDE79qE5wt

Protocol No. XVI

> We will obliterate from the memory of the people all those facts pertaining to former centuries which are not to our advantage, leaving only those which emphasize the mistakes of the GOY governments. The study of practical life, of obligatory social order, of the interrelationship of human beings, the avoidance of evil, egotistical examples that plant the seed of evil, and other questions of a pedagogical nature, will head the education program.
>
> We will abolish all unlicensed teaching. Students will have the right to gather, with their relatives, in their colleges as if in clubs. During these gatherings, on holidays, the teachers will read supposedly unbiased lectures on problems of human relationship, on the law of imitation, on the cruelty of unrestricted competition, and finally, on new philosophical theories which have not yet been disclosed to the world. We will promote these theories into dogmatic beliefs, using them as stepping-stones to our faith.

TEDx is a prime example of this aspect of Protocol No. XVI. It is an intellectual platform that people around the world can utilize to express the latest and greatest intellectual ideas that the world should follow. Some discussions are of practical use. However, TEDx is an academic platform used to legitimize the darkest and most evil behavior one can imagine. They intellectually justify every Babylonian Talmudic behavior one can think of—everything from pedophilia to cannibalism.

TEDx—Jonas is a Pedophile
bitchute.com/video/Kz4u3S0UzNdo

Richard Saul Wurman, the Jewish founder of TED Talks, and Frank Gehry (born Goldberg)

TEDx—How Young Blood Might Help Reverse Aging [Cannibalism Justification]
bitchute.com/video/hFkJWjmDeFZo

Now that we have taken a good look at the Jews' goals and their playbook, we need to examine their modus operandi. The next chapter will build off of the information we learned in this chapter and help us understand how the Jews implement the goals in their playbook.

JEWS ARE THE PROBLEM!

3

MODUS OPERANDI OF THE JEW: THEY WAR BY PROXY

Now that we know what the Jews want and how close they are to getting it, we need to understand how they go about carrying out their plans. This is critical. Securing our survival in the 21st century will involve a 3-phase process:

1. Unmasking—*Jews: Knowing Who They Are and How to Identify Them*
2. Modus Operandi—*Understanding How the Jews Carry Out Their Plans*
3. Collision—*Permanently Ending the Jews' Reign of Terror on Planet Earth*

This book unmasks the Jews by identifying them by what they are currently doing to **YOU**. We reference many resources that provide historical analysis of Jews and their history around the world. However, we will only focus on the history of Jews in this book to the degree it helps us understand their current efforts to enslave and/or exterminate us.

This chapter focuses on how the Jews operate. We will provide a behavioral analysis of the Jew that will likely cause them serious palpitations. You will learn what to expect from them based on their interests. You will also learn how to predict what their interests are and might be in the future. Lastly, you will learn how to spot this invisible force based on the dynamics of an otherwise normal environment.

First, we need to know what things to expect from the Jews in relation to any socio-political dynamic and/or conflict. The following list of Jewish characteristics are foundational to understanding their modus operandi:

1) Jews are *always* on both sides of the issue!
2) Jews war by proxy.
3) Jews are notoriously greedy and dishonest.
4) Jews are incorrigible. They push for their desired result without regard for consequence.
5) Jews fight to usurp, infiltrate, or destroy any potential social force that presents itself.
6) Jews are the masters of false flag operations. They use them to execute proxy wars.
7) Jews seek to control every relevant narrative in society.

Jews are Always on Both Sides of the Issue!

This is one of the most important characteristics about the modus operandi of the Jews. If you do not know and understand this concept, you will never understand this group. In order to always maintain plausible deniability for evil, they make sure there is a Jew on every side of any relevant issue. In this way, no matter which side wins, they can claim they were on the "good" side. Also, when their hand of evil is shown, they can quickly point to the Jew on the "good" side and say, "It is not *all* Jews . . . (random good Jew) did this and that on the good side." This tactic also allows them to prove their value. They make significant contributions to each side such that they become almost invaluable.

This value affords them the leverage to influence the direction and/or outcome of any conflict. In many instances, they accomplish this by serving as lawyers representing both sides of a dispute. So, they are enriched while controlling the argument of both sides. It is like being the promoter, hype-man, and referee in a boxing match. You have significant influence on who wins the fight. And more importantly, you get rich no matter the outcome.

Jews War by Proxy

Jews are not usually the frontline militia for their wars. They architect and engineer conflicts; however, they prefer to get the *goyim* to physically fight their battles against the *goyim* or other Jews. In this way, they can hide their bloody hands and often manage to never be seen at all.

Jews are Notoriously Greedy and Dishonest

Jews have a perverse lust for money and profit that makes them some of the worst business partners. Their Babylonian Talmudic faith reduces all non-Jews to the status of exploitable slaves; thus, they feel no guilt in lying to and stealing from the *goyim*.

Jews are Incorrigible. They Push for Their Desired Result Without Regard to Consequence

Jews do things no other group would believe they would get away with. This is part of what makes them so successful and effective. Even in the face of certain exposure, they push forward right in front of the victims' faces. They are convinced the stupidity of the *goyim* outweighs the risk of our backlash against their evil designs. This is why they publicly stole an election in front of the American public despite any concern of the consequences. This is why they openly censored a former standing president of the United States of America. Their attitude is, "What are these idiot slaves going to do about it?" This personality characteristic has historically been viewed as egotism by victims of Jewish abuse and consequently led to pogroms against them.

Jews Fight to Infiltrate, Usurp, or Destroy any Potential Social Force that Presents Itself

Jews do not believe in competition. They firmly believe in their total dominion over the planet. As a result, any potential power base they do not control is viewed as a conflict. This is true regardless of whether or not there is any known conflict or opinion of Jews.

Jews are the Masters of False Flag operations. They Use Them to Execute Proxy Wars

A false flag operation is a scheme whereby one party commits an attack of violence against a second party and blames it on a third party. The purpose is usually to make a public villain out of the person or group accused of the attack. 9/11 was a Jewish-controlled false flag operation. The purpose of it was multifaceted. It was executed to:

1) Eliminate the freedoms of the U.S. Constitution through the USA PATRIOT Act
2) Launch wars against Israel's enemies in the Middle East
3) Establish the foundation for using "security" as the justification for government invasion of privacy and high-tech electronic surveillance designed to make slaves of Americans and the world

Even though it was orchestrated by Jews at high levels, they convinced the world it was organized and executed by Arabs. Most people believe it to this very day. For more information, watch:

Missing Links Video on 9/11 & Israeli False Flag Operations
911missinglinks.com

Jews Seek to Control Every Relevant Narrative in Society

This aspect of their personality is at the root of how they transitioned from publicly stealing the 2020 presidential election directly into launching the genocidal "plandemic" scheme, The Fauci. They used heavy-handed censorship tactics to create one international narrative and systematically discount, hide, or defeat all others. Their monopoly of media made this possible. Jews controlled the narrative so well that American citizens never asked the obvious question: "What is the best way to fight a bioweapon?" It certainly would not be a vaccine. But the conversation never got this far. The entire world was herded in the direction of accepting harmful technology injections, from the same source who made the original bioweapon, as a solution to fighting bioweapon attacks. It is unreal when we think about it.

But it all happened in front of our faces while the MSM publicly admitted the injections would not stop people from getting or spreading the sickness. Again, the obvious question is: "If the injection does not stop me from getting or spreading the sickness, then it is not a vaccine, and since you have informed me it is not a vaccine, then ***what are these injections?***"

Basic truth and logic are swiftly discarded to the wind when Jews implement hardcore censorship. They use their control of the narrative to "lead the sheep to slaughter."

Civil War to Garvey: Jewish Modus Operandi in the U.S. (1861-1925)

Jews have had a rough experience throughout the history of Europe. In each case when the host countries somehow discovered their parasitic ways before being eradicated, Jews faced some form of backlash. Sometimes it was expulsion. Other times they were liquidated and had their property and businesses seized. And still other times they were physically assaulted and killed. The problem they always ran into was that once they were discovered, there was no distraction they could produce to stop the European (non-Jew) response. They were met with well-earned and well-deserved hostility. Nevertheless, their incorrigible attitude has allowed them to continue to prosper in Europe to the degree that today, they are actually in a position to eradicate White European non-Jews from the continent. And they are in the process of doing it.

America was different. The presence of Afrikan (Black) people in America was a great gift to the Jews. In fact, it was not a gift; they organized it.

The Secret Relationship Between Blacks and Jews Vol 1
socialarchitects26.com/The-Secret-Relationship-Between-Blacks-&-Jews-1-$20-p454422058

Our presence in America provided a permanent tool for distraction away from their exploitation of Anglo-Saxon Americans. The slavery culture of the South made being White, poor, and hopeless OK as long as you were "better than a Black person." The concept makes no sense. But it is still very much part of the psychology of America today. White and Black people in America know this is true. What we do not realize is this is an idea planted by the Jews to keep White folks' attention off of them. It is a psychological proxy war designed to focus Anglo-American hatred on the subjugation of Black people as their priority—despite their condition. Jews have used this to their advantage. Any time Anglo-Saxons got wind of Jewish parasitic encroachment on the freedoms of this Republic, Jews instigated a pogrom against Black people using Anglo-Saxon Americans as the proxies. In this way, Jews have used Black people in America as red herrings for White Anglo-Saxon abuse and violence. This problem got worse after the Civil War.

Let us start by examining a brief history from the Civil War in 1861 through the rebirth of the Ku KKK in 1915. This will provide a sense of how the Jew operates. To begin, there was significant Jewish influence on both sides of the Civil War. The North had influential and wealthy Jewish integrationists, and abolitionists like Charles Sumner and George Stearns supporting and financing the Union efforts. A Jew named Judah P. Benjamin, often called "The Brains of the Confederacy," was the second-in-command of the Confederacy in the South. He also became the Secretary of State for the Confederacy. An obvious question should arise from these facts: Which side were the Jews on during the Civil War? The answer will take us back to #1 in our Jewish Characteristics list above. **Jews are always on both sides of the issue!**

In the case of the Civil War, it was no different. The group who financially benefited most from the enslavement of Black people in America was Jews. They financed the Transatlantic Slave Trade. They owned the routes, the insurance companies, the major slave ports, the largest plantations, many of the auction blocks, etc. They had everything to lose from the ending of slavery. And they were deeply embedded in the culture of slavery in the South. Some of the most ardent racists in the South during antebellum America were Jewish.

At the same time, many of the Northern Jews were concentrating on creating a central bank to totally control U.S. currency. They saw no need for chattel slavery because a free Black population would create a permanent distraction base to activate anytime they were planning a major move against the Anglo-Saxons. To this end, many of the Northern Jews financed the Union Army and helped recruit Black soldiers. Implementing the Rothschild-conceived Federal Reserve System, a private bank owned by Jews, was the central banking system concept Northern Jews were focused on during the Civil War.

A Brief History of the Rothschild Family & How They Operate
bitchute.com/video/RoHsYybCnG45

If the North won the Civil War, the Jews wanted to have enough influence to ensure the creation of a Jewish-controlled central banking system. If the South won the war, the Jews wanted to have enough influence to ensure the creation of a Jewish-controlled central banking system. As a result, the Jews financed both sides of the war. None of them on either side cared about freeing Black people from the tyranny of slavery. They were interested in the tyranny of a Jewish-controlled central bank in America.

The unscrupulous and sheisty behavior of Jews did not go unnoticed. U.S. General Ulysses S. Grant expressed his discontent with the Jews during the war. In fact, they were so notorious for *economic and political corruption* that Grant issued General Orders #11 banning all Jews from the Department of Treasury:

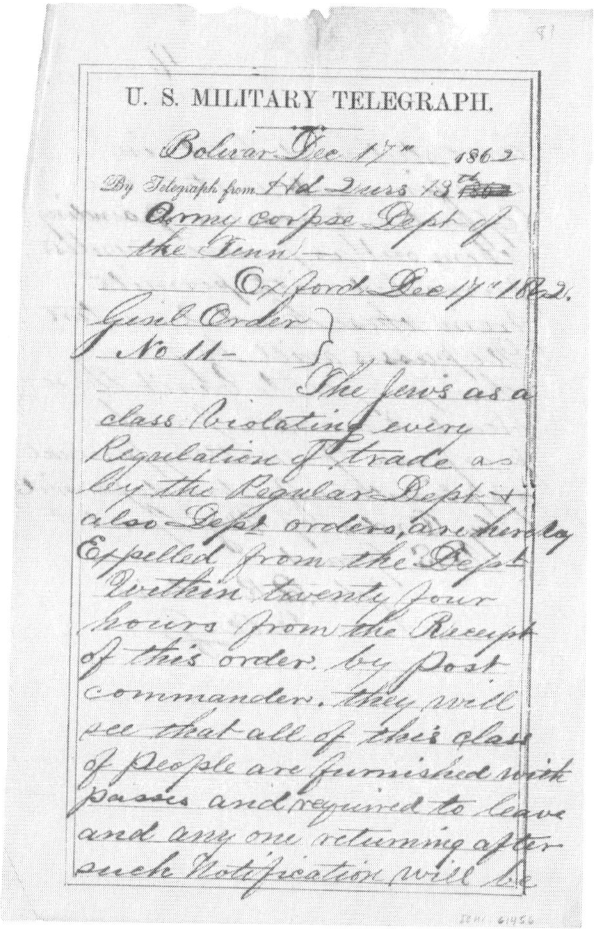

U. S. MILITARY TELEGRAPH.

Bolivar Dec 17th 1862

By Telegraph from Hd Qrs 13th Army Corpse Dept of the Tenn—

Oxford Dec 17th 1862.

Genl Order No 11—

The Jews as a class Violating every Regulation of trade as by the Regular Dept & also Dept orders, are hereby Expelled from the Dept within twenty four hours from the Receipt of this order. by Post commander. they will see that all of this class of People are furnished with passes and required to leave and any one returning after such Notification will be

General Orders, No. 11.
HDQRS. 13TH A.C. DEPT OF THE TENN.,
Holly Springs, December 17, 1862.

The Jews, as a class violating every regulation of trade established by the Treasury Department, and also department orders, are hereby expelled from the Department within twenty-four hours from the receipt of this order.

Post Commanders will see that all of this class of people be furnished passes and required to leave, and any one returning after such notification will be arrested and held in confinement until an opportunity occurs of sending them out as prisoners, unless furnished with permit from headquarters.

No passes will be given these people to visit headquarters for the purpose of making personal application for trade permits.

By order of Maj. Gen. U.S. Grant:
JNO. A. RAWLINS,
Assistant Adjutant-General.

Later the same day of Orders #11, General Grant wrote an explanation for this order to his Assistant Secretary of War:

To Christopher P. Wolcott
Head Quarters, 13th Army Corps.
Department of the Tennessee
Oxford, Dec. 17th 1862
HON. C.P. WOLCOTT
ASST. SECTY OF WAR
WASHINGTON, D.C.

Sir:

I have long since believed that in spite of all the vigilance that can be infused into Post Commanders, that the Specie regulations of the Treasury Dept. have been violated, and that mostly by Jews and other unprincipled traders. So well satisfied of this have I been at this that I instructed the Commdg Officer at Columbus to refuse all permits to Jews to come south, and frequently have had them expelled from the Dept. But they come in with their Carpet sacks in spite of all that can be done to prevent it. The Jews seem to be a privileged class that can travel any where. They will land at any wood yard or landing on the river and make their way through the country. If not permitted to buy Cotton themselves they will act as agents for someone else who will be at a Military

> post, with a Treasury permit to receive Cotton and pay for it in Treasury notes which the Jew will buy up at an agreed rate, paying gold.
>
> There is but one way that I know of to reach this case. That is for Government to buy all the Cotton at a fixed rate and send it to Cairo, St Louis, or some other point to be sold. Then all traders, they are a curse to the Army, might be expelled.
>
> I am, Sir, Very Respectfully
>
> Your Obt Servant
>
> U.S. Grant
>
> Maj Genl.

General Grant was one of the few Anglo-Saxons in the history of America to use his power to take direct action against the Jews. I believe Grant was on his way to the full expulsion of the Jews from the United States of America. This would have changed everything. And had Abraham Lincoln not countermanded Grant's actions on January 4, 1863, he might not have been assassinated.

If Grant had expelled the Jews from the country, they might not have been able to create the Federal Reserve. But the Jews escaped America's wrath and pushed to achieve their plans.

Once the Union won the Civil War and Reconstruction began, the Jews were in a quagmire. Lincoln put the U.S. on Greenbacks (printing our own money) which was in direct contradiction to a privately owned central banking system. So, the suspected Jew, John Wilkes Booth, murdered President Lincoln. At that point, the Lincoln problem was solved.

After Lincoln was murdered, the Jews had another problem. Afrikans in America under Reconstruction were using our skilled labor to build towns throughout the South. Recently freed Black men and women built entire towns and governed them during the period from 1865-77. Black people were protected in the South by Union soldiers. This allowed us enough freedom to enjoy the American dream for 12 years. These 12 years were the glory days for many Black people; but they were a nuisance to the aims and objectives of the Jews.

Black people controlled skilled labor. We could now charge for work we had mastered over the past 250 years when we did it for free. We had our own economies. We were quickly becoming a separate economic force within this Republic. If the Jews allowed Black people to become fully independent and self-sufficient, they would have to conquer two separate nations of people, White and Black. They would have to compete with Black labor, which was absolutely impossible to do fairly during this period. And if Black people became an independent respectable class, the Jews could not easily and effectively use us as distractions from their designs.

Mind Your Black Business **(3-DVD Set)**
Hard Copy through USPS Mail
socialarchitects26.com/Mind-Your-Black-Business-Series-3-Disc-DVD-Set-p19079915

In 1867, two years after the end of the Civil War and after their conception, the KKK visited Judah P. Benjamin in England. Benjamin loved what they represented so much that he financed the KKK to purchase costumes, weapons, supplies, and horses to reign terror on newly freed Afrikans in America. This history is captured in a book written by Susan Lawrence Davis, daughter of a founder of the Alabama KKK. The book is entitled, *Authentic History: Ku Klux Klan, 1865-1877*. "In 1867, Bishop Richard H. Wilmer, who was a close friend of General Morgan, the Second Dragon of the Realm of Alabama, went to England and there he saw Judah P. Benjamin who had been a member of the Confederate States Cabinet . . . Mr. Benjamin's interest in the Ku Klux Klan was so aroused that he borrowed money and gave it to Bishop Wilmer to buy horses, saddles, fire-arms, and other necessities for the Ku Klux Klan." (Davis, p.40)

The irony. It is because of Jews the KKK rose to prominence and became the domestic terrorist organization Black people have come to despise.

Not only did Jews finance the rise of the original KKK, but they helped broker the deal that ended Reconstruction, legalized domestic terrorism against Black people, and instituted a form of oppression in the South that rivaled chattel slavery. On that fateful date of Monday, February 26, 1877, at the Wormley Hotel in Washington, D.C., Jewish U.S. Representative William M. Levy (D-LA) helped broker a deal, called the Compromise of 1877, to elect Rutherford B. Hayes as president over Samuel J. Tildan. Part of the deal allowed Hayes to get the presidency in exchange for his promise to remove federal troops from the South where they were protecting the Constitutional rights of Black people from groups like the KKK.

The agreement was reached and Levy was selected to sell the deal on the floor of Congress. On Thursday, March 1, 1877, Levy delivered the most memorable speech given on the subject. His speech laid the foundation for the end of Reconstruction and the **legalized permanent oppression** of Black people in America.

The Compromise of 1877 can rightly be seen as the foundation for the modern use of the term "racism." As used in America, *racism* is meant to describe the post-Reconstruction *system of law* and *organized White oppression* against Black people in America that replaced slavery. We were no longer in *chattel slavery*. Jews intentionally trivialize this reality, to include anyone as potential victims of racism, in order to prevent people from properly perceiving the obvious and consistent abuse Black people endure in this country. The ugly reality is that Jews architected much of it themselves.

Directly following the Civil War, Jews financed the rise of the KKK. Jews undermined Reconstruction and returned Black people to a form of slavery today called, "institutional racism."

And Jews intentionally stole the one economic industry Black people dominated in America: skilled labor.

A Jew named Samuel Gompers (born Gumpertz) founded the American Federation of Labor (today AFL–CIO) in 1886. The practice of dominating and controlling labor is an important piece of the Jewish playbook. They try to take control over labor in every country they sink their hooks into. They use this control as a means to drive people towards civil unrest when they deem the time appropriate. More than any other factor in American history, we may view the founding of the AFL as the reason why Black men do not control skilled labor in America today. Jews *intentionally* took the mastery our forefathers had developed in working skilled labor trades for free under the institution of American slavery for 250 years, and systematically criminalized Black men's right to practice these same trades through free enterprise. It was prohibited for Black men to join the AFL. However, it was also prohibited to hire skilled labor without going through the AFL. This was a death sentence for many Black men during the late 1800s. Skills that had been passed down for generations and allowed Black men who possessed them the ability to go into business for ourselves, were thrown into the

American dumpster of unrealized hope and freedom for Afrikan people. The Jews created a new wave of unemployment that never needed to exist. After all, what good was transferring a skill to your son that he could not use to make a living? We had the skills and the desire to use them; but we did not have the answer to Jewish manipulation of Anglo-America.

It is important to note that not all Anglo-Saxons went along with this Jewish-sponsored death sentence to Black self-employment. Some Southerners wanted the best quality work at the best price. No one could beat the Black man's work or price at that time. Some of these White folks were outright murdered when they hired Black men to do work against the AFL mandates.

"The AFL formed in 1886, with its leadership being the imported product of Jewish union activism in Europe . . . Under Jewish founder and president Gompers, the AFL successfully bludgeoned industrialists into a Whites-only hiring policy that would come to characterize the labor market for the next century." (*Secret Relationship Between Blacks and Jews* Volume 2, p. 311)

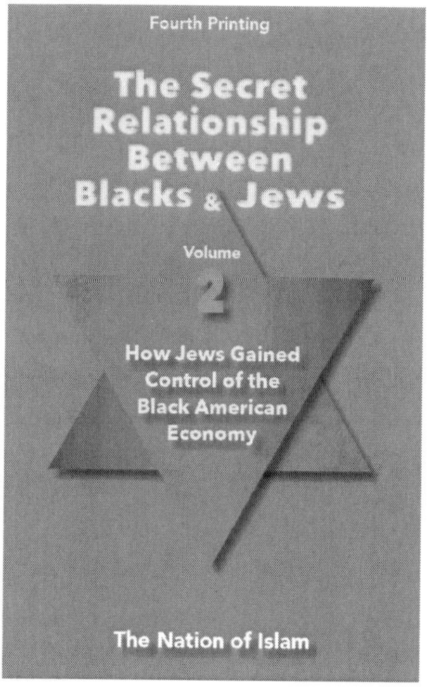

The Secret Relationship Between Blacks and Jews **Volume 2**
socialarchitects26.com/The-Secret-Relationship-Between-Blacks-&-Jews-2-$20-p257225316

As mentioned previously, Jews financed the rise of the KKK, undermined Reconstruction, replaced chattel slavery with "racism," and ran Black people out of skilled labor. Jews also founded the National Association for the Advancement of Colored People (NAACP) to destroy Booker T. Washington's efforts at revitalizing Black skilled labor and to take control over the Black sociopolitical landscape.

By 1890, Washington became the primary leader of Black people in the U.S. He worked diligently to produce institutions for the advancement of our race. He focused on trade schools and agricultural schools to provide Black students with means to go into business for ourselves and build our own communities. He was phenomenal at convincing wealthy Anglo-Saxons to finance his vision for Black self-development in the skilled trades. He was not fond of the Jews because he saw them as exploiters who were harmful to the interests of Black people in America.

From page 200 of *Anti-Semitism in America* by Leonard Dinnerstein:

> . . . as late as the 1890s a friend [of Washington] cautioned him to keep his prejudices about Jews out of his speeches. Washington seems to have thought of Jews as exploitative shopkeepers and usurious creditors and from time to time differentiated between the Jew and the white man. However, disparagement of the Jews was impolitic since a number of them in the North made substantial financial contributions to black causes. As [his biographer] noted, "in [Washington's] effort to secure donations to his school . . . it was in his interest to drop his prejudice." Publicly he did so and many of his twentieth-century writings, in fact, praise Jews.

But in private, he expressed a different view. In a 1904 note to his business manager, Washington ordered him to buy supplies "whenever possible from Gentiles": "In looking over our bills from Montgomery, I very much fear that we are getting our trade too much centered in the hands of a few Jews. Whenever we can get equally fair treatment in prices and quality of goods from persons other than Jews, I prefer to have our trade scattered among them. In creating public sentiment in favor of the institution the Jews cannot be of much service." (*Booker T. Washington in Perspective: Essays of Louis R. Harlan*)

Washington was prophetic. The Jews would not have any interest in seeing the people they systematically evicted from the skilled trades return to these industries. They would only support Washington in order to gain leverage to shut his efforts down later. But Washington had such a good relationship with the wealthy Anglo-Saxons in America that the Jews could not attack him directly. So, they did what they are prone to do. They warred against Washington by proxy.

In 1909, Mary White Ovington, Oswald Garrison Villard, William English Walling, and Dr. Henry Moscowitz created the NAACP. The NAACP was founded by Jews and their associates in order to take control of Black sociopolitical affairs in America. They used a few Anglo-Saxons and Black people as proxies; but it was entirely contrived by Jews. The Jews then pit W.E.B. Dubois and others against Washington in an effort to stifle his efforts at pushing Black people towards economic self-sufficiency and independence.

The Jews wanted to keep Black people economically dependent so they could exploit our reliance on White benevolence for sustenance. They knew Anglo-Saxons would resist integration with Black people violently, and this would afford them the ability to assimilate themselves into arenas where they were commonly excluded, while causing bloodbaths for Black people pushing for integration. It would also allow them to act as attorneys on both sides of the arguments. Jews could represent the rights for Anglo-Saxons to enforce the Jim Crow laws that came out of the 1877 Compromise; and they could represent the Black people who they got to join their NAACP organization who were seeking integration. **Jews are always on both sides of the issue!**

Leo Frank, the ADL, & the Federal Reserve

The year 1913 was very pivotal for America.

Amendment XVI to the U.S. Constitution, allowing Congress to levy an income tax, was ratified on February 3, 1913.

In April of that year, Leo Frank, a Jew in Atlanta, Georgia, molested and murdered a 13-year-old White girl named Mary Phagan. He tried to blame it on a Black man, but his attempt did not work. He was tried, found guilty of murder, and sentenced to death by hanging. In many ways, Frank was the Jeffrey Epstein of his time. This was the most popular child rape case in the South of its day. Jews saw Frank's reputation as a sexual predator and child murderer as an image that could harm the group. As a result of his guilty verdict, the Anti-Defamation League (ADL) was founded in September 1913 to protect the image of Jews in America that was tarnished by a Jewish pedophile child murderer who they still support to this day. This almost reads like something out of a novel entitled, *Tales of the Babylonian Talmud*.

The plot thickens. On December 23, 1913, the Jews convinced Woodrow Wilson and the Congress to pass and sign into law the Federal Reserve Act of 1913. Abraham Lincoln lost. The Rothschilds got their central banking system and America was sentenced to financial doom.

Between 1913 and 1915, the Jews lobbied the governor of Georgia to commute Frank's death sentence. Surely enough, on June 21, 1915, Governor John Slator commuted Frank's death sentence with the intention of eventually seeing Frank walk free. Fortunately, the hands of justice prevailed. On August 17, 1915, a well-organized group of White vigilantes withdrew Frank from prison, drove him hours away to a prepared location, and hung him from a tree.

Though this was a temporary victory for most parties involved, the victory was short lived. For while the Anglo-Saxons were waiting for Frank to receive his death sentence, and Black people were making songs about how horrible the murder of Mary Phagan was, the Jews were up to their dirty tricks. In 1914, D.W. Griffith started filming *The Birth of a Nation*. This film took the story of Reconstruction, perverted it, included the molestation and murder of a fictitious

Mary Phagan lookalike, but changed the culprit from a Jew to a Black man (White man in Blackface). The film so deeply touched the hearts of White America that the KKK was reborn—larger than ever.

Leo Frank, "The Only Righteous Lynching in U.S. History"
Child Rapists & Murderers Should Hang!

On February 18, 1915, in the same year the film was released by the Jew, Louis B. Mayer of MGM Studios, it was shown to President Woodrow Wilson in the White House. This film alone was responsible for sparking the rebirth of the most notoriously violent domestic terrorism organization against Black people in America. And it was done by Jews distributing the first blockbuster film in the history of this country, *The Birth of a Nation*, as broadly as they could.

Ku Klux Klan marching in Washington, D.C. (September 13, 1926)

The sadistic thing about this change of events is it was carried out by White Anglo-Saxons, but architected by Jews. In order to take attention from Jews in Southern factories exploiting child labor, sexually violating women, and Leo Frank's rape and murder of a child, they decided to stop the defaming of their group. But instead of changing their behavior, they used sophisticated propaganda to condition already-racist White Southerners to redirect their resentment away from the Jewish perpetrators and onto Black men. Now, without one single act of abuse by a Black man, Anglo-Saxon Americans became petrified that we were going to rape and kill their women. And the results were tragic.

Booker T. Washington transitions on November 14, 1915. Upon his departure, the Jews took full advantage of this incredible vacuum in Black national leadership. And with the release of *The Birth of a Nation* in the same year, the impact was magnified. Where was a Black leader who could effectively ease the tensions of White America and ensure them that this movie was only slanderous propaganda? Who could convince them that Black men had no desire to target White women for sexual violence and conquest? Black America was left in a terrible predicament.

Will Brown lynched in Omaha, Nebraska false accusation of rape (September 1919)

From *The Birth of a Nation* until this very day, White American men have the idea in their minds that Black men have some kind of unbridled thirst for the rape and exploitation of their women. A lot of this fear is based solely in Jewish propaganda that works. We know it works because at the same time the Jews were using propaganda in America to ignite another state of domestic terrorism for Black people, they were plotting to get a homeland in Palestine. They made an agreement with England to bring America into World War I (WWI) in exchange for land in Palestine. England agreed by signing a document known as the Balfour Declaration.

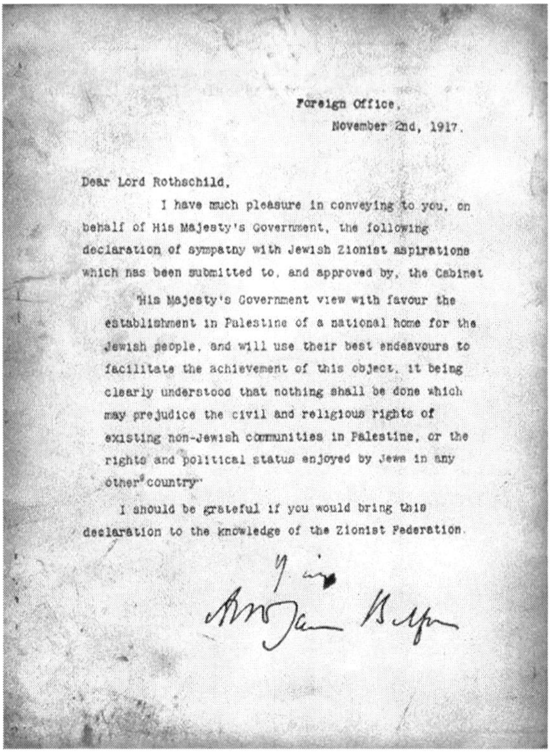

Foreign Office,
November 2nd, 1917.

Dear Lord Rothschild,

I have much pleasure in conveying to you, on behalf of His Majesty's Government, the following declaration of sympathy with Jewish Zionist aspirations which has been submitted to, and approved by, the Cabinet

"His Majesty's Government view with favour the establishment in Palestine of a national home for the Jewish people, and will use their best endeavours to facilitate the achievement of this object, it being clearly understood that nothing shall be done which may prejudice the civil and religious rights of existing non-Jewish communities in Palestine, or the rights and political status enjoyed by Jews in any other country"

I should be grateful if you would bring this declaration to the knowledge of the Zionist Federation.

Yours
Arthur James Balfour

Balfour Declaration

In order to get the U.S. into the war, the Jews in America started an anti-German media campaign that made Americans believe Germans were a nation of demonic terrorists. It was so effective American retail stores would later ban all German-made goods. Before this time, America was Germany's major trading partner. At the snap of a finger, the Jews turned Germans into America's enemy.

Woodrow Wilson became the true puppet of the Jewish international power brokers. He gave America's economic future to the Jews via the Federal Reserve. He sold Black people's lives to the KKK in order to defend the Jewish image. He sent American troops to die in WWI to support the Jews stealing land from the Palestinians to build a home base for themselves.

His efforts also helped the Bolsheviks overthrow Russia, which caused a major genocide of Europe's population and an explosion of Marxism and communism in the East. Both are fancy terms for Zionism (Jewish hegemony).

Europa **Part 2**
bitchute.com/video/mZbWENURHTDV

So, while the Jews were busy destroying Black economic self-sufficiency and creating pogroms for us here in the West, they were also taking control of the U.S. economic lifeline—its money. And at the same time, they were in the East starting wars to exterminate White Europeans and securing a home base.

They got Anglo-Saxons to terrorize and fight Black people in America. They got Black people through the NAACP to fight Whites and knock down doors for Jewish entry into areas they were previously denied access. They used Americans against Germans to take a homeland. They turned Russians and Germans against one another in a series of bloodbaths. They were very busy during President Wilson's time in office.

The Black Messiah: Marcus Mosiah Garvey

By the early 1920s, the most celebrated Black leader in the history of America was thriving. His name was Marcus Mosiah Garvey. He was an extraordinary orator with the power to move Black people across the planet. Mr. Garvey had the largest Black self-help organization in the history of the Western world, the Universal Negro Improvement Association (UNIA). His message was for the unification, upliftment, and self-sufficiency of the Black race. He was met with savage indignation by the Jews. Baba Garvey's sentiment for Jews met their ire with ire:

> He [Marcus Garvey] considered them "spies for the rest of the white race" and saw them as a brake on the black man's self-

reliance and a hindrance in the quest for black nationalism. In a speech entitled "Beware of Greeks Bearing Gifts," he said:

> The greatest enemies of the Negro are among those who hypocritically profess love and fellowship for him, when, in truth, and deep down in their hearts, they despise and hate him. Pseudo-philanthropists and their organizations are killing the Negro. White men and women of the Moorfield Storey, Joel Spingarn, Julius Rosenwald, Oswald Garrison Villard, Congressman Dyer and Mary White Ovington type, in conjunction with the above-mentioned agencies, are disarming, dis-visioning, dis-ambitioning and fooling the Negro to death. They teach the Negro to look to the whites in a false direction . . . at the same time distracting the Negro from the real solution and objective of securing nationalism.
>
> (*Race First,* Tony Martin, p. 274)

Mr. Garvey clearly understood Jews were using the NAACP as a front to achieve their own ethnic objectives and a tool to inhibit Black self-sufficiency. Unfortunately, the Jews worked in conjunction with Black integrationists/homosexuals, mulattoes, and the federal government to destroy Mr. Garvey and UNIA. The judge—a Jewish leader in the NAACP—Julian Mack was one of the most prominent Jews in America. He was the president of the Zionist Organization of America and the World Jewish Congress, secretary of United Jewish Charities, and president of the American Jewish Congress. The prosecutor on his trial was also a Jew. And six out of the 12 jurists were Jewish. He was convicted on trumped up charges of mail fraud and sentenced to five years in prison in 1923, served two, then was deported to Jamaica in 1927.

The major issue of concern for the Jews in relation to Marcus Garvey was his working relationship with the KKK. Garvey was a proponent of Black Racial solidarity and he understood the KKK wanted the same thing for their people. He was no friend of the Klan. However, he respected their honesty better than the trickery of the Jews. In his words:

> Between the Ku Klux Klan and the Moorfield Storey National Association for the Advancement of "Colored" People group, give

> me the Klan for their honesty of purpose towards the Negro. They are better friends to my race, for telling us what they are, and what they mean, thereby giving us a chance to stir for ourselves, than all the hypocrites put together with their false gods and religions, notwithstanding. Religions that they preach and will not practise; a God they talk about, whom they abuse every day—away with the farce, hypocrisy and lie. It smells, it stinks to high heaven.
>
> —Marcus Mosiah Garvey (*Race First*, Tony Martin, p. 344)

Many of the White separatists, which might be considered patriots today, agreed and consequently worked with Mr. Garvey. This is a quote from one such individual, Earnest Sevier Cox, of the White America Society: "A black man who advocates racial integrity cannot be opposed by a white man who advocates racial integrity. They are drawn to each other, for they fight in a common cause." (*Race First*, Tony Martin, p. 344)

This working relationship between the Honorable Marcus Mosiah Garvey and the White Nationalist community frightened the Jews. It represented a possible return to the Union Army Civil War alliance between Afrikans in America and Anglo-Saxons. This union threatened to help both races move towards separation and self-sufficiency and isolate the Jews as the problem in America. Since the Civil War, this was a preoccupation of the Jews in America. It has always been their worst nightmare—Black and White Militants shaking hands to fight against them. They would be absolutely doomed in America and have to figure out where to flee for asylum.

To avoid this deadly cocktail for ending Jewish hegemony in the world, they organized their homosexuals and integrationists in the Black community to help bring the momentum of UNIA and Marcus Garvey to an effective halt. In doing so, they severed the dialog between Black Nationalist groups and White Nationalist groups for a long time. To some degree, we do not dialog to this very day. And when we do interact, it is with Whites as the masters. It is seldom, if ever, independent Black leadership and independent Anglo-Saxon leadership dialoging about common interests. This is illegal in Western Israel.

The greatest benefit of dialog in today's world would be survival.

The Jews are openly committing genocide against both races in real time. No two groups are more familiar with their tactics, have been fighting them longer, have successful histories of resisting Jewish terrorism, and have the personalities necessary to target their genocidal aims for destruction. We also control major world populations that could restrict their ability to escape the wrath of justice and regroup to continue their agenda. Enough Black people are smart and resilient and enough Whites are experienced, mean-spirited (as demonstrated by how they righteously dealt with Leo Frank), and prepared for this to be a problem for the Jews.

The Bolsheviks:
Stop the Blacks in the West, Kill the Europeans in the East

Communism as a political system burst on the scene in Europe with the violent murder of Czar Nicholas II of Russia and his family in 1917 by the Bolsheviks. The prominent leaders of the Bolshevik Revolution were Jews. Vladimir Ilyich Ulyanov (alias Vladimir Lenin), Karl Heinrich Marx, Leon Trotsky (born Lev Davidovich Bronstein), Lazar Moiseyevich Kaganovich, and Genrikh Grigoryevich Yagoda, were all ruthless Jewish extremists.

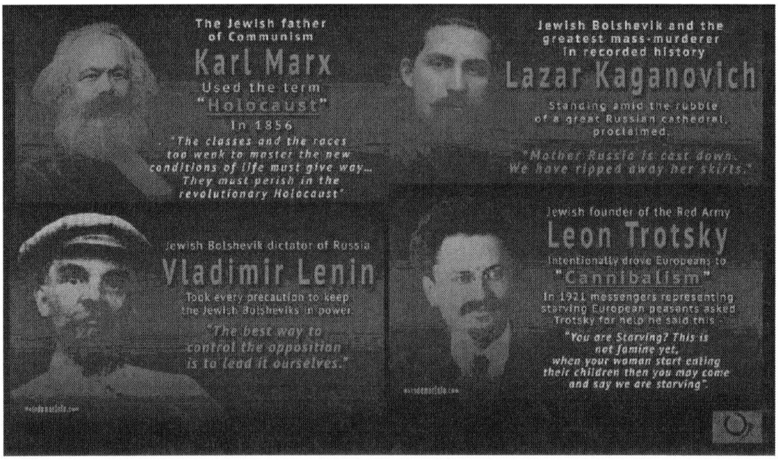

Jewish leaders of the Bolshevik Revolution (aka Russian Revolution)

When the Bolsheviks overthrew Russia in 1917, they unleashed the type of tyranny and slaughter that rivals other more popular genocides in the history of the world. They systematically disarmed, starved, raped, hunted, tortured, mutilated, and exterminated millions of Russians. When the Bolsheviks rounded up the Russian farmers' food stocks at gunpoint, they left the country starving. Russians became so desperate they began to eat their own babies. Between 1917 and 1960, it is estimated the Jews orchestrated the slaughter of an estimated 66 million Russians.

The interesting thing about the Bolshevik Revolution is it was funded by many Jews in the West—some working on Wall Street in New York. While the Jews were sponsoring the KKK domestic terrorism assault on Black communities in America, they were simultaneously committing active genocide against White people in Eastern Europe. The same Jews who opposed UNIA were supporting the Jewish overthrow of Eastern Europe. At the same time the Jews were instituting the Federal Reserve in America, they were *"finding"* money to finance revolutions in Eastern Europe.

In America, the Jews used Anglo-Saxons as the battering ram to stifle and collapse Black self-development and progress. They also used Black people as battering rams for Jews to integrate into the White American power structure. In Europe, they used White Anglo-Saxons like Winston Churchill as battering rams to help the Jews besiege Eastern Europe.

This reality is troublesome. It means the Jews can simultaneously attack multiple groups, each significantly outnumbering them, in different corners of the Earth. It also strongly suggests the Jewish implementation of the Federal Reserve was not just a financial power move; it was actually a means for Jews to fund their world overthrow agenda using American money. So Americans had to pay interest on our own money in order to finance the murder and starvation of Russians—the same nation that supported Abraham Lincoln in preserving the Union. It was Czar Alexander II of Russia who sent a fleet of ships to the West and East Coasts of America in support of the Union Army. He did not want to see America taken over by the Rothschild banking cartel. We cannot make this up.

The Birth of Modern "Entertainment": Jewish Modus Operandi in the U.S. (1831-present)

The last historic Jewish American phenomenon we will discuss in this chapter is the birth of the modern entertainment industry, which can fairly be traced back to the late 1820s and a suspected Jewish individual named Thomas Dartmouth Rice. He was called an "Ethiopian Delineator," which was a fancy word for Minstrel of Blackface actor. This is when Whites would paint their faces with Black polish and mock Black people. This became the predominant form of "entertainment" in the country through the 1920s.

Thomas Dartmouth Rice, "Father of Black Face"

Rice painted his face Black and dressed like an enslaved person. He copied a dance off of a crippled Black man called the "Jim Crow" dance. It would later be classified as "Jumping Jim Crow." He charged audiences around this country to come and watch him imitate this crippled Black man's dance. It became a social and economic hit.

The disrespect and racial insult in the portrayal is obvious. But the political motivation for what it grew into became far more relevant and dangerous. Blackface became the standard for American entertainment. The social ramifications were that it targeted Black people's self-esteem and sense of beauty. It also made Anglo-Saxon Americans lose any semblance of respect for the value of Black life. Many Anglo-Saxons in the North had minimal contact with Black people because slavery was not as prevalent in the North as in the South by the 1820s. Seeing these filthy depictions through traveling Jewish live play performances and circuses became a national pastime. It became a way to spend the weekend with one's family.

The circumstances leading to the Civil War had already begun to materialize. One of the issues that would ultimately have to be resolved was slavery. Rice's Blackface Jim Crow performance was a psychological tool used to justify keeping Black people in America in bondage. The idea was to portray Black people as happy slaves who did not want and could not manage our freedom. It became believable because the American portrayal of "Black culture" was 100% under the controlled narrative of the Jewish manipulators of the public's mind.

You heard it correctly. ***The American entertainment industry is a psychological warfare system designed by Jews to keep Black people enslaved.***

As Black efforts for abolition increased, so too did the Blackface portrayals and the modern entertainment industry blossom. These depictions of Black inferiority were 100% contradictory to the strength and majesty of the Black abolitionists and freedom fighters of the mid-1800s like Henry Highland Garnett and Martin Delany. These were brilliant historians, writers, orators, and warriors. They were men and women whose entire lives were spent uplifting a downtrodden race of people and moving us to freedom from chattel slavery. Some of them, like Baba Martin Delany and Mama Harriet Tubman even fought in the Civil War.

The Great Martin Delany

It is important to note, the Jews did not stop with Blackface traveling minstrel shows, plays, and circuses; but they also put Blackface images into sales ads and cartoons. These images destroyed the image of Black people around the world and helped nurture the attitudes that supported the Berlin Conference and colonialism in Afrika.

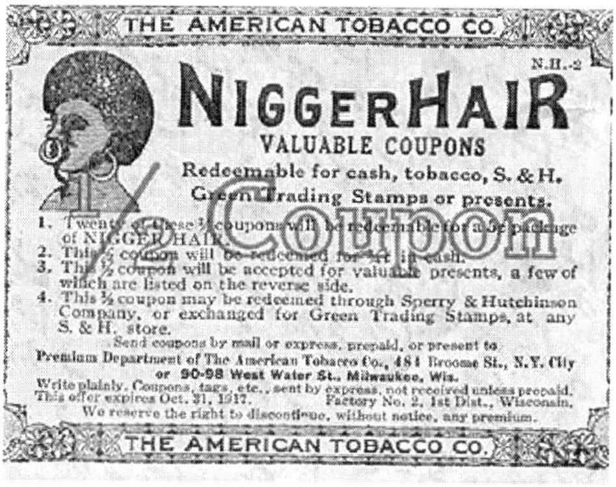
THE AMERICAN TOBACCO CO.
N.H.-2
NIGGERHAIR
VALUABLE COUPONS
Redeemable for cash, tobacco, S. & H. Green Trading Stamps or presents.
½ Coupon
3. This ½ coupon will be accepted for valuable presents, a few of which are listed on the reverse side.
4. This ½ coupon may be redeemed through Sperry & Hutchinson Company, or exchanged for Green Trading Stamps, at any S. & H. store.
Send coupons by mail or express, prepaid, or present to
Premium Department of The American Tobacco Co., 481 Broome St., N.Y. City
or 90-98 West Water St., Milwaukee, Wis.
Write plainly. Coupons, tags, etc., sent by express, not received unless prepaid.
This offer expires Oct. 31, 1917.
Factory No. 2, 1st Dist., Wisconsin.
We reserve the right to discontinue, without notice, any premium.
THE AMERICAN TOBACCO CO.

NIGGER HEAD TEES

"I took CALIFORNIA FIG BITTERS last night."
Oh my?
plums
peaches
AND
green corn
Tips
guess this will fix me.

LITTLE AFRICAN
A DAINTY MORSEL

NEW!
NIGGER JOE'S
1900's
TAR SOAP
PRICE
5 cent
Black soap fo' black faces!

The New Improved
NIGGER BOY
Steel Wool
SOAP PADS
the SOAP is IN the PAD
the SOAP is IN the PAD
IT'S SO EASY

Remember, it was Blackface propaganda from *The Birth of a Nation* in 1915 that sparked the rebirth of the KKK and the steep rise in lynching and racial violence against Black men in America.

A scene from The Birth of a Nation (1915)

A scene from The Birth of a Nation (1915)

Blackface is the historical root of American entertainment. *And since modern entertainment was started for the purpose of keeping Black people enslaved, one can surmise Blackface is the basis for the Jewish psychological propaganda against all groups.* For Hispanics, it is Brownface. For Asians, it is Yellowface. For Whites, it is Whiteface. And if they ever decide to attack one of their own, it will be Jewface. Whatever face it is, the rules are the same. Decide someone is a monster. Paint an image of them being a monster. Tell people how to feel about the monster. Tell them what should be done to the monster. Then find a way to get whatever their true objective is at the expense of the monster.

By the 1920s, nationally syndicated radio programs like *Amos 'n' Andy* which had two White guys, at least one of whom was Jewish —Freeman Fisher Gosden—portraying buffoonish Black characters, fed the appetite for Black disrespect and hatred in America. At the same time, Jews like Al Jolson (Lithuanian Jew, born Eizer Yoelson), Eddie Cantor (Russian Jew, born Isidore Itzkowitz), George Burns (Polish Jew, born Nathan Birnbaum), Sophie Tucker (Russian Jew, born Sofiya Kalish), et al. were seen painted in Blackface roles disrespecting the image of Black people. They even recruited children like Shirley Temple into this racial image terrorism.

Amos 'n' Andy (Gosden & Charles Correll)

Shirley Temple in Blackface

Well into the 1940s, cartoons like *Coal Black and De Sebben Dwarfs* were shown throughout the country. These cartoons are very telling.

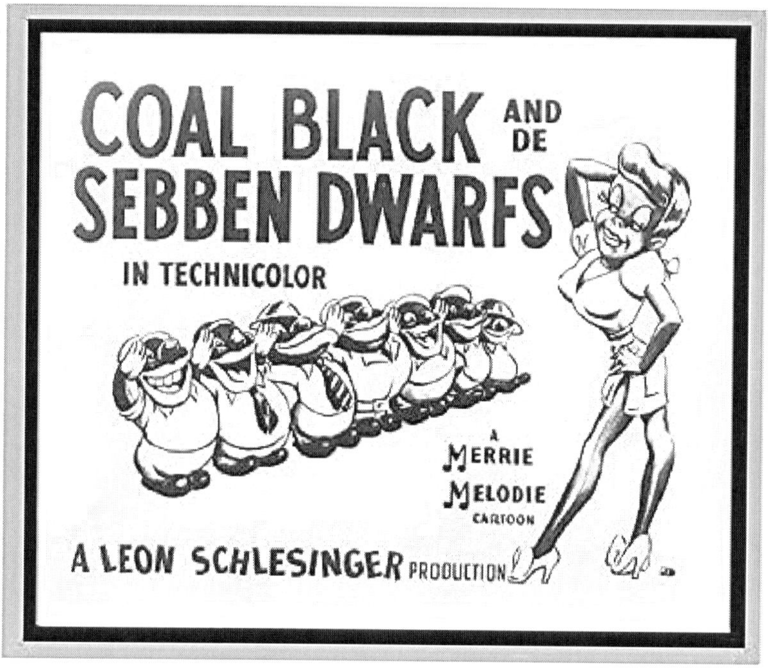

Coal Black and De Sebben Dwarfs

When we originally saw these negative depictions of our Black image from the 1820s through the 1920s, we thought it was Whites trying to destroy the image of Black people in America in order to justify keeping us in a second-class citizenship status. In recent times, we discovered the true Jewish aims reached much deeper.

But, it wasn't "Whites." It was specifically the Jewish mind orchestrating a literal transition from the perverse concepts of who and what we are as Afrikan people into our people actually internalizing and becoming those very same images. They achieved this by eventually paying Black people to "act" like the images Jews created and wrote scripts for. They made these Black people rich and spread these images around America and the world.

Ethnic Notions (1986)
bitchute.com/video/AdinU6EzPMHS

By the mid-to-late-1900s, Jews got to the point with media of being able to fathom an idea in their mind, project Black images acting out those ideas, get Black people to accept and covet those ideas as our own, and ultimately see Black people become living manifestations of the ideas they originally fathomed. Here is an example from page 54, of Dr. Nathan and Julia Hare's classic book, *The Endangered Black Family: Coping with the Unisexualization and Coming Extinction of the Black Race*: "(1976) Late in the spring, about 500 black women hold a conference at the Berkley YWCA House. The hidden agenda expressed by conference leaders and voiced openly at the climax of the meeting is to find a way for black women to begin to find alternatives to black men. The answers proposed are: white men and homosexual reinforcements [i.e., lesbianism]."

The idea to separate the Black man and woman was conceived in the mind of the Jew. (We haven't researched it, but I am confident Jews sponsored similar conferences for Anglo-Saxons encouraging White women to leave their men.) The Jew introduced these ideas into social groups, women's groups, and academia throughout the country, etc. Then the Jews decided to attack this objective with their big guns—Hollywood. They made a huge breakthrough in 1985 with the movie *The Color Purple*. This film was a masterpiece of revisionist history and social destruction. It set in motion a definitive cultural shift for Black women to spiritually, emotionally, and physically abandon Black men. They used Oprah Winfrey, a Black woman who they groomed (Jeffrey Jacobs, the Jew responsible for Winfrey's success), to swap the roles of men and women in a relationship. They used Whoopi Goldberg to capture the emotion of Black women who were either victims of past abuse or had low self-esteem to show Black women that lesbianism was the better alternative to Black men.

Turning Black women away from Black men was their obvious goal. Jews took the idea and expressed it through paid Black actors in *The Color Purple*. The idea Black women "Don't need a [Black] man" became a standard in Black culture after this film. Moreover, the idea that lesbianism became perceived as acceptable cultural behavior for Black people, when we had *always* viewed it with hostility since ancient times, is amazing in such a short period of time. This single production was so successful in helping destroy the relationship between Black men and women, they keep remaking it in film, Broadway musicals, plays, etc., to this very day.

And as they are wont to do, they used a book written by a Black woman as the proxy for this horrible production. When you read *The Color Purple*, it has almost nothing to do with the film except the name of the book and the characters. But the Jews hide their agenda behind the fact the author and all the actors were Black. So, unless a person investigates the production team, the Jewish hand will never be seen.

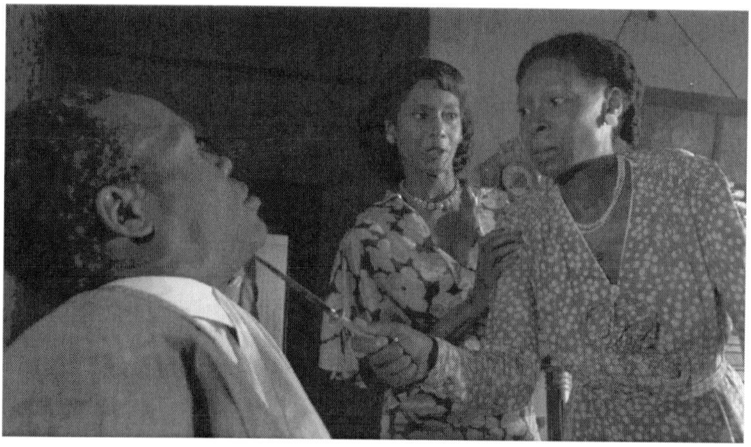

The Color Purple (1985) by Steven Spielberg

In more recent times, they used the television program *Scandal* to encourage Black women to abandon Black men and become the sexual toilets for powerful White men. In many ways, it glorifies the master-slave relationship Black women actually experienced for over 250 years during chattel slavery. But through the magic of Jewish media, the rape and torture of a "slave winch" in real slavery, has been turned into something fashionable and desirable among many Black women. And the upgrade from *The Color Purple* to *Scandal* is that the executive producer for Scandal is Shonda Rhimes. This gives a Black woman the leverage to create our own destruction while the Jew stands all the way back and says, "It was totally produced by a Black woman. It is her work." But we all know who owns the studio and the network. The Jews have now groomed Black men and women like Lee Daniels of *Empire* and Shonda Rhimes of *Scandal* to take over the creative license of Black cultural destruction through mass media genocide. This is sophisticated proxy warfare.

Scandal closet sex scene

These productions sound different but they really are the same. Some Jew had the intention of causing dissension and separation between Black men and women. They started the plan in motion through various mechanisms of society. Then they used MSM to provide visual examples of how we should carry out this agenda. They made it look and sound thrilling and exciting. They groomed Black people to come up with our own scripts to enact the cultural genocide. And they stood back and clapped at the success of the design. They laugh in great hysterics as Black people celebrate the "success" of these productions, having no idea we are championing our own extermination. We actually publicly call ourselves "nig*ers."

Remember the excerpt from Protocol No. XV:

> They long for the emotion of success and for the applause which we grant them lavishly. We create their success in order to utilize the self-deception that is born with it and by which people, without noticing, begin to follow our suggestions without suspecting them, and being fully convinced that their infallibility originates its own ideas and, therefore, does not need those of others. You have no idea how easy it is to bring even the most intelligent GOYS to a state of unconscious credulity, and, on the other hand, how easy it is to discourage them by the smallest failure, or merely by ceasing to applaud them, thus bringing them into servitude for the sake of achieving new success. *To the same extent as our people ignore success for the sake of carrying out their plans, so are the GOYS ready to sacrifice all their plans for the sake of success.* Their psychology makes the problem of direction easier for us. Those tigers in appearance have the souls of sheep and nonsense filters through their heads.

Shonda Rhimes, executive producer of Scandal

Even though I am using examples of how they target Black culture for destruction, it is plug and play. Whatever race you are, just pick the Jew-facilitated program, change the players' names, and copy and paste the above. It works on all of us.

This is critical for our understanding. In order for the Jews to successfully exterminate people on the planet, they must be able to undermine and destroy family and culture. When groups do not have strong families, they cannot defend themselves in times of war. Babylonian Talmudic pathological family dysfunctional narratives and psychopathic sexual perversion properly inoculated into media have proven to be incredible tools for Jews to destroy cultures.

They can take an insane idea and get people to accept it as an actual cultural practice through media cognitive conditioning and repetition. They can convince people to love their enemies and hate their friends through media. They can create new realities through media. *The Color Purple* and its impact on Black male/female relationships is one of the best examples.

Geraldine character from the Flip Wilson Show (1970)

Another example is what the Jews did with Black male homosexuality. When I grew up in the 1980s, the worst thing you could be on the planet was a homophile. By 1970, Jews started putting Black men in dresses (transvestites) on national television. We thought the idea was to effeminize the Black male, and to some degree it was. But they actually intended to get Black people to accept and embrace this perversion as part of our culture. In 2022, former NBA star Dwyane Wade and popular actress Gabrielle Union are jointly raising his son as a girl. *A Black man in America is actually supporting his own biological son being raised as a girl!* After decades of presenting Black men on major media platforms dressed as women, the Jews have manipulated society to such a degree they can now convince men to promote this behavior onto our own sons. Much of this transition occurred slowly with the help of MSM.

From left, Dwyane Wade, his son Zion, & Gabrielle Union (2021)

Brother Nathanael—*Who's Funding and Spreading the Transexual Movement*
realjewnews.com/?p=1539

The modern MSM is the most powerful psychological weapon system in the history of the world. The same system the Jews used to orchestrate the destruction of Black sovereignty in the U.S., tear down and redefine Black culture and family values, confuse our Black self-identity, and redirect Black aspirations, is the same system being used to facilitate their destruction of the planet.

For instance, President Donald Trump caught the elite off guard when he won the 2016 election. That was not in the plans of the "Western Jews." By Western Jews we mean to distinguish between Jews who live in and directly control America and Europe, and the "Eastern Jews," who live in and control Israel and the Far East, like Chabad Lubavitch. Trump was backed by the Eastern Jews who helped him defeat the Western Jews (who control Western media) in the election. So, the Western Jews unleashed the most aggressive and abusive media campaign ever launched against a sitting U.S. president. He faced four solid years of relentless bad press, including lies and slander. Trump was turned from a popular entertainer into one of the most reviled people on this planet, overnight.

To be clear, the election of Trump over Hillary Clinton was an internal fight between Western and Eastern Jews. Either result was a loss for the *goyim*. It is only a case of the lesser of two evils, where Trump was the lesser.

Now, the Jews have decided President Putin will be viewed as the worst creature on planet Earth. Through their variety of psychological indoctrination tools, they present him to Anglo-Saxon Christians in America as Satan. While President Putin is busy trying to protect his country and essentially the entire world from this modern Jewish Bolshevik overthrow, his own American White brothers and sisters are calling for Russia to be nuclear bombed. White anchors on FOX News are calling for President Putin to be assassinated. Terribly unthoughtful and uninformed American citizens are volunteering to go to Ukraine and fight the trained Russian military. In the middle of an impending food crisis and hyperinflating gas prices, Americans are sending money to the Ukraine government, whose bioweapon labs worked with the Wuhan lab that made the bioweapon now called The Fauci (COVID-19). Americans are funding our own genocide while the people fighting against those who're working to exterminate us are trying to tell us to wake up.

In closing this section of the chapter, too many of us are tuned into the psychological warfare system tools such as MSM news, television, radio, film, pornography, etc. Too few of us are seeking alternative sources for credible information. This book is designed as a resource tool for clarity in seeing who is behind the problems on planet Earth today.

Analysis: Jewish Modus Operandi & How to Pierce Through Our Cognitive Dissonance

As a Black man, it feels like some type of bad movie. I have spent my entire life seeing domestic terrorism first hand from White Americans. I have studied it, taught it, and resisted it. I thought I had an incredible grip on the Anglo-Saxon psyche. I concluded Whites were inherently prone to hate and attack Black people without provocation. The last three years have made me question exactly how much power Jews have over the minds of people—even White Anglo-Saxon racists.

Jewish Control of the Anglo-Saxon American

I have watched White folks in America be told to hate and go kill Whites in Russia and receive it with the same enthusiasm they justify torturing and murdering Black people. I have watched the racists on FOX News turn against members of their own race because the Jews told them to. This is bizarre because I would have said, "If it was a White country like Russia, they would not do that. They only do this in Afrikan countries." But I would have been wrong. Apparently, White folks will do it in any country the Jews tell them to. And as I think back on the Obama era, Jews got White folks to line up by the millions to vote a homosexual mulatto into the highest office in this land, the presidency.

And it is not only psychological control Jews hold over American citizens. They exercise extreme levels of control over the leadership in this country. By mid-March 2022, the Jews were trying to pressure

Biden to declare a "No Fly Zone" in Ukraine which would be an "act of war" that would launch the traditional phase of WWIII. Biden refused to do this, then publicly advocated for Israel as a member of NATO to openly side with the West in the conflict with Russia. Within a few days, Biden's son Hunter made the news for his laptop that showed sexual and financial misconduct. The information on this laptop was ignored by MSM for months. After Biden publicly pressured Israel to take a position on the war in Ukraine, the laptop contents immediately became news. We have not heard any more requests from the Biden administration for Israel to take a side in the conflict with Russia. These types of threats to destroy a person's entire life are how the Jews use leverage to get leaders around the world to do their bidding. When incorruptible leaders like President John Magufuli of Tanzania arise, they do not like it. Jewish mind control over the Anglo-Saxon and control over their leadership is real.

Jewish Control of the Afrikans in America

Unfortunately, Black people do not appear to be any more independent in thought than Anglo-Saxons. I watched Black people who have a historical hatred for homophilia, witness a White man running for president grope and molest little children in front of their eyes, and then go out to stand in line to vote for him. These Black people did not feel bad voting for someone who I personally showed them videos with him publicly molesting children. They celebrated when he was awarded the presidency even after I told them he would force them to take harmful injections.

Now that this same pervert nominated a Black judge with a documented history of giving light sentences to convicted pedophiles, Black people fought for this woman to become a Supreme Court justice. Many found ways to defend her pro-pedophile record. It feels like the entire world is upside down. She is not even married to a Black man. The most outspoken members of our community have *always* been against interracial marriage. This is one thing we have always had in common with White Nationalists. But this interracial phenomenon has been so thoroughly normalized through the media weapon system, that people feel guilty wanting to continue their race in reproducing itself. Yes! I am blaming Jews for convincing people that racial suicide is healthy.

Jewish Purpose for Unregulated Immigration

We should also look at illegal immigration today. After Black people fought to knock down barriers to Black progress in America by pushing for the Civil Rights Act of 1964, the Jews went into action. They got the Immigration and Nationality Act of 1965 passed the next year. It took until now to see where the Jews' long-range planning was headed. Simply stated, Jews orchestrated the collapse of the American Republic partly by using immigration of non-White persons from around the world. In the current environment, the Hispanics are the Brown people who are a major focus of this effort. But they are not the only foreigners being invited. The U.S. recently imported 100,000 Afghanis and 100,000 Ukrainians. All this is happening while illegal immigrants entering through Mexico are crossing the border like they are crossing the street.

So, when Anglo-Saxon White Americans complain they are being displaced and exterminated, they are correct. I always believed they were just complaining because they did not have the same power they have traditionally held in America. That could be a part of it. But no matter how you look at it, they are being displaced and exterminated. And the system of White supremacy as we have understood it is being dismantled before our eyes. Look at the statues of Confederate generals and the like being torn down throughout this country. Look at Saudi Arabia refusing to answer calls from a president of the United States of America. White supremacy as a standing system of Anglo-Saxon authority over the lives of Black people is dying. If it was not being replaced with Jewish hegemony and mass extermination, this would be a good thing for Afrikan people. As it stands, we are stepping out of the frying pan directly into the fire.

Jewish Control & Funding of the Gay Lesbian Movement (GLM)

Black Lives Matter (BLM) is a modern-day version of the NAACP with a homophile twist. The reason the Jews financed this movement was to use a Blackface front to push homophilia in the Black community and use Black people as the face for their overthrow of White Anglo-Saxon America. The three Black female leaders of BLM (Alicia Garza, Opal Tometi, and Patrisse Cullors) are all feminists/ lesbians. Garza (Schwartz as a child), who coined the term in 2013, considers herself Jewish because she grew up with a Jewish stepfather. She was married to transexual woman Malachi Garza (White transexual woman who wants to be a man). BLM was primarily funded by Jews including George Soros (born György Schwartz). Jews used the outrage and momentum of the Black youth in Ferguson, Missouri, who were fighting against the unjust murder of Mike Brown, as fuel to propel BLM to prominence. This feminist, homosexual, Zionist, anti-Black man and anti-Black family movement was given significant airtime on all of the mainstream liberal media outlets. In fact, CNN made BLM an extension of their official URL. The financing of this movement was exclusively Jewish and served exclusively Jewish interests. There was never anything authentically Black about it except the Black people who supported it, not knowing its true purpose.

BLM should more accurately be called JAM, Jewish Agendas Matter.

Alicia Garza (BLM Cofounder) on Laura Flowers Show

truthout.org/video/building-movements-without-shedding-differences-alicia-garza

Jews Sponsoring Proxy Wars Between White People and Black People for Their Agenda

Critical Race Theory and the transgender homophile agenda are the two biggest American school system controversies of our time. They are both being sponsored by the same group. As opposed to listing each individual involved in this process, I want to elaborate on these two phenomena in a different way. The reason is because it is more important for this book to teach you how to identify this group when you do not have hard evidence than when you do. You cannot be certain nor publicly blame them for things you have not confirmed; but you can identify their presence in most instances and use your instinct and logic as a basis to begin your investigation and research.

To understand CRT, it is best to look at the two agendas together. In short, CRT is a basis for curriculum that identifies Anglo-Saxons in America as racist by birth. It seeks to get White folks to acknowledge their innate racist tendencies and deal with the pain and suffering they have caused different races of people. It is specifically aimed at Anglo-Saxon children in schools.

The homophile agenda seeks to confuse and sexualize children by exposing them to the LGBT sexual sickness prevalent in the U.S. today. It teaches children there are more than two genders. It teaches children they can change their gender. It even tries to convince children to have surgery to change their gender. A few questions will help cut through the war between Black people and Anglo-Saxons as to whether CRT is right for public schools.

Question 1: Do Black people in America want the transgender homophile agenda pushed in the schools with their children?

Answer 1: No.

Question 2: Do Black people in America have the power to implement CRT nationally in the public school system?

Answer 2: No.

Both White and Black people agree on stopping the transgender homophile assault on children in schools. Black people do not have the power to implement CRT in the schools. The only two questions left for discussion are:

1. Who had the power to implement CRT into the public school system?
2. Why did they implement CRT into the public school system?

The title of the book answers the first question: *Jews Are The Problem*
The second question is answered by the other agenda that both races agree on. We are both hostile against pushing homophilia on children. In order for the Jews to push this perverted agenda in schools to our babies, they must maximize Black/Anglo-Saxon racial tension. Otherwise, both groups would swarm on this agenda like locusts. And if we saw that both Black and Anglo-Saxon communities felt similar about this perversion, we would begin to ask ourselves, "Who is doing this?" Then we might draw the same conclusion we are making here.

The strategy in this case was to use both Black people and Anglo-Saxons as proxy fighters to focus on the racial issues with CRT while they cleverly push the LGBT sexual perversion agenda on children in schools. This was a brilliant strategy that played on realities that are not maturely discussed. By preventing mature Black people and Anglo-Saxons from engaging in constructive dialogue about our disagreements, Jews can easily create problems that increase the enmity between the groups.

In this case, the year 1840 can help us see the picture better. The Anglo-Saxon who is asked about 1840 begins to think about their family history and what their great, great grandparents were doing at that time. You think about the glory days. It can cause a bit of nostalgia.

When a Black person hears 1840, we think, "Hell no. I ain't going back. We can end this conversation right now."

As a result of this reality, it is ridiculous for Americans to think Black people are going to share the same opinion of this country as anyone else. We did not have the same experience as anyone else. And we still do not have the same experience as anyone else—even though the gap is beginning to shrink due to the Jews' maneuvers.

When your White forefathers were blazing a trail for a free Republic, we were the contradiction in the process. We were fighting for our very lives.

This is the result of history. What Jews do is take this scenario and say:

> Let's create a curriculum that appeals to Black people's desire to express how horribly America has treated them. And we'll use a Black interpretation of White racism and aggression to frame it. Then we'll unleash it into the school system training White children to see themselves as inherently racist. When the White parents react, we'll put Black spokespersons up to articulate how correct the CRT curriculum is and why it's so necessary. We'll position the Black community to essentially taunt and antagonize the Anglo-Saxon community with these ideas and begin to draw the racial animosity and ire we've sown into their psychology over the generations. Whites will be waiting for the moment to explode on the Black people who are celebrating and believe themselves to be enforcing this curriculum. The more both groups resist the LGBT agenda, the more we'll intensify the discussions of CRT to keep them distracted and separated. Predictably, at no point in the process will any of the *goyim* have any idea we are the invisible force driving this debacle.

The object of the entire process is to gain complete sexual access to the children while simultaneously preparing Anglo-Saxons for a hard, anger-driven strike against Black people in America. Then, the Jews will broadcast the White racism for the world to see and finance Black gays into the streets. If strong Black men enter the picture, the Jews will choose to either depict us as terrorists or freedom fighters. White folks and Black folks will be out in the streets at war with one another, never realizing it was the Jews who put this entire set of events in motion. And the fight will derive out of the emotions created by the Jews via CRT, and not a tangible racial grievance either group has towards one another.

This works. Each group, Black and Anglo, is a proxy to fight the other group in a war against the children of both groups.

Jews Are The Problem

What I am beginning to honestly evaluate is how much power the Jews have over the minds of everyone. Americans of all races are incredibly suicidal and self-destructive in today's environment, and most of it is because the Jewish system of mind control and manipulation is so sophisticated, they can give us any message that is harmful to us, in a way we believe is our own independent thinking, and then get us to carry out our own demise without ever suspecting anything. In fact, we will argue to the point of a fist fight that nobody convinced us to do anything. It was all our idea, no matter what the idea is. They also commit the most heinous crimes imaginable and never have it tied to them being Jewish. We all know something terribly wrong is happening; but we create terms that cause us to remain confused and unclear as to what or who is causing the problems. Either we create terms—or maybe we have terms created for us. It becomes hard to tell.

Points to Ponder

Remember, there will be Jews who fight against every problem stated in this book with passion and vigor. But the one thing they will never do is tell us it is the Jews causing the problems. This becomes a challenge for many in accepting the truth in this message. If they have a Jewish friend, colleague, neighbor, attorney, etc. who is truly committed to fighting against some evil that exists, we still have to ask ourselves, "Is this a good Jew, or is this a Jew playing the good side of the fence in case the Jews get busted?"

The reason I bring this up is because it is very important. The cleverest trick the Jew has played is in the creation of their most valuable proxy. Jews use people, communities, races, and even nations as proxies. It is what they do. Right now, Ukraine is the proxy to draw NATO into a war with Russia and their allies in the East.

But their most powerful proxy is the one we never see. It took me years to figure this out. It is by far their most sophisticated trick. I watched it for decades and never quite understood it. And one day it hit me like a ton of bricks. The Jews' most powerful proxy is

YOU and ME. What I mean by this is that through religion, education, media, support, financial contributions, and many other means, Jews have cleverly conditioned the entire world to magically pop up to their defense, even in the absence of any Jews to defend themselves.

It first starts in our own heads. Someone accuses a guilty Jew of wrongdoing and we instinctively block the suggestion that this could be due to their group dynamic. And either we, or someone else in the room, says "It is not all Jews." This sounds reasonable until you consider we do not do that for any other group to the same degree. For instance, whenever I make generalizations about the KKK, no one ever stops me to discuss the good Klansman. I am sure in many groups when Anglo-Saxons talk about Black people wearing our pants too low, no one fights with vigor that "It is not all of them." But whenever Jews are mentioned as a group for their wrongdoing, it is usually Gentiles who jump up to defend them. Through Christianity, they have made themselves mini-gods via their biblical interpretations. But even non-Christians tend to come to their defense. Jews have shrewdly and methodically implanted the defense for themselves, even in their absence, in the minds of the very people they are exterminating.

This is why some people asked themselves if they should read this book, even though we all know something is wrong today. And we sense that Jews have something to do with it. Yet we still have a caution about diving into the issue. Why? Because the Jews have systematically turned us all into proxies over the course of time. Somehow, we get convinced that we cannot analyze information for ourselves and draw our conclusion from our own set of determining factors. We can only explore that which the Jews have made it OK to consider. But we do not know that we are living in Proxy Land. Hence, anyone who tries to bring up anything about the Jewish involvement in world affairs is immediately attacked.

Jews should be expected to try to prevent being discovered by any means at their disposal. In this instance, Jews *are not* the problem. *We have to deprogram ourselves.* We cannot be the defense mechanism for the genocidal maniacs who are actively exterminating us. If they will be defended by anyone, it must be the "good Jews." In my book, the only mechanism for measuring a "good Jew" is the one who acknowledges that the truth in this book is true, and will lead the way in stopping their own people from exterminating the planet. This means they must share every piece of relevant information on who is doing it, how they are doing it, and the best way to stop it.

This may sound harsh, but so what. My race being exterminated is much harsher!

Let us wrap it up.

Jews create a problem and/or take advantage of a problem that already exists. Then they figure out how to exploit the problem and gain profits. At some point, they make a decision to create a conflict to get two or more groups ready to fight one another. Then they find a way to partner with both sides. They make sure to take control of the narrative so the only thing people understand about the conflict is what the Jew tells them. It never matters if it is true or not. It only matters that the Jew is telling the people what to think.

Once the Jew has full control of the narrative, they intensify the conflict by either instigating the parties into physical battle or by executing a false flag operation that will definitively create physical conflict. They then fund both sides of the war effort and keep it going until they have squeezed all the value out of the conflict. Once they have destroyed the host(s), they move on to the next conquest.

Remember, these hosts can be people, groups, nations, minds, husbands and wives, animals, races, businesses, etc. The Jew will exploit anything that can be exploited.

All this is being done with an ultimate goal of mass extermination. So, no matter how big or small the scenario, the Jew will try to use it as a means to achieve the ultimate goal of Jewish world hegemony. Anything and everything they produce or steal from others, will be weaponized and used against the goyim in the interest of Jewish World Hegemony.

Anyone the Jews work with who is not one of them is a proxy to be discarded at their convenience. No matter what side of any conflict you find them, they are always only on one side.

The side of the Jew.

JEWS ARE THE PROBLEM!

4

JEWISH IDENTITY THEFT OF AFRIKAN HISTORY

The most ironic aspect of the "Jewish Question" is that they are not actually Jews at all. The Euro-Asiatics, who commonly refer to themselves as "Jews" in today's world, are actually Ashkenazim and Sephardim. These are two different groups of Euro-Asiatics who had no place in the development of the ancient world. Neither group had any relevant history linking them to the time when the pyramids were built, nor the development of the mighty dynasties in Kemet, called Egypt today.

Furthermore, Judaism is a religious system whose principles derive from ancient Afrikan civilization, as do almost all religions. Why is this the case? It is because Afrikan people were the first people on the planet. This is a historical and a scientific fact proven through mitochondrial DNA. When we look at Kemet, we are looking at one of the best-preserved representations of ancient Afrikan civilization.

No one questioned the "Blackness" of Kemet in ancient times. The word "Kemet" actually means "Black Land" or "Land of the Blacks." And because there were no Jews controlling the narrative during the first 25 Dynastic Periods (3100-656 B.C.), the entire world respected the richness and magnificence of Black civilization. A Dynasty is a family line of rulership. When rulership of the kingdom was taken over by a new family, this was the beginning of a new Dynasty.

The reality of history is Black people laid the foundation for civilization and ruled the ancient world. Jews aside, Europeans have ruled civilization since the 1500s, and in the 21st century, they and Asians dominate modern civilization. These are assessments easily made by studying history with an open mind. The question of who did what and when, is one that can be greatly fulfilling to anyone seeking this type of truth.

The difficulty of making these basic assessments in the modern context is piercing through the eye of "racism White supremacy" which stands on the footstool of Jewish hegemony. The Jews have stolen the Afrikan civilization identity and claimed it for themselves. In order to keep up the farce, they have fueled Anglo-Saxons to be resistant to acknowledging Black civilization to the point of complete denial. They do this by offering Whites the platform of "racism White supremacy" as a temporary place of dominance over Afrikan people worldwide. In order to justify the continued mistreatment of Black people, Whites feel the need to believe Black people have never accomplished anything. This eases White guilt and allows them to comfortably oppress and abuse Black people.

For this very reason, Jews create every message and narrative imaginable to support the idea of Black inferiority and worthlessness. They constantly push the notion Black people come from a history of savages and wandering nomads. This targeted assault on the truth of Afrikan history and civilization is foundational to their use of Anglo-Saxon aggression against the rise of any Black nation or community. It is also foundational to their lie they are "God's Chosen People" and therefore the founders of civilization.

The concept of being God's Chosen People did not originate with the Jews. The oldest documented records of this concept are on the ancient temples in Kemet. Afrikan people got to a point in civilization where we believed leaders were appointed by the Creator. Each *Suten* (King) wanted to prove he was worthy of the throne. This meant being divinely appointed by the Almighty to govern over the well-being of the kingdom. One of the most popular *Suten* in the history of Kemet, Ursa Maat-Ra Setep En Ra Ra-Messu Meri Amen (better known as Ramses II or Ramses the Great), had the words Setep En Ra, "Chosen by God," in his very name. Part of his royal *shenu*, the oval text holding his royal name, is shown on next page:

Ursa Maat-Ra Setep En Ra Ra-Messu Meri Amen's royal shenu

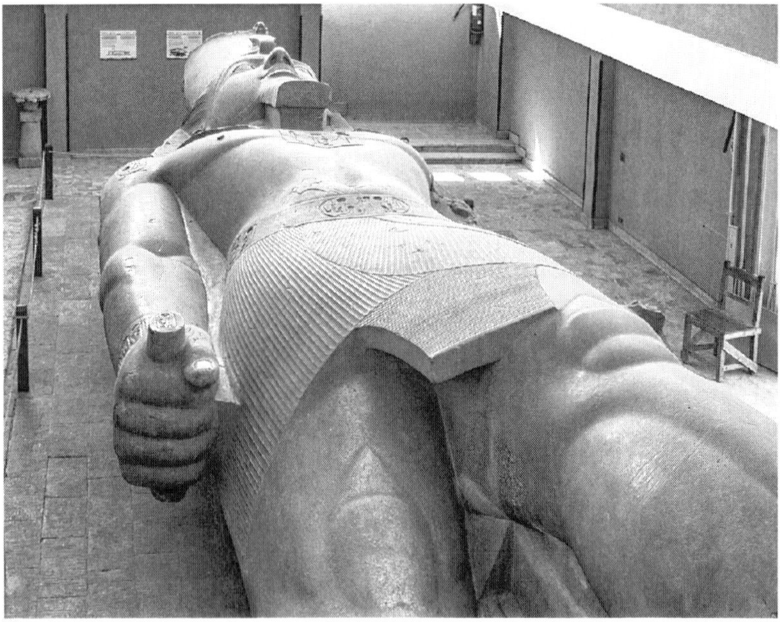

Statue of Ursa Maat-Ra Setep En Ra Ra-Messu Meri Amen in Kemet

These Black men were the envy of the world during their time. We gave language, agriculture, science, mathematics, architecture, construction, engineering, astronomy, astrology, art, dance, music, writing, farming, and so much more to the world. Our Ancestors were magnificent. And their contributions to early civilization are undeniable.

Nevertheless, all the great accomplishments we produced in the history of the world amount to little in the determination of our current condition. Whites can fairly claim a dominance in modern technology which can be viewed as modern civilization. This is a reasonable and honest assessment. However, for their goals and objectives to be achieved, the Jews cannot afford reasonable and honest assessments.

The entire Jewish identity is predicated on the theft of Afrikan history. They have magically inserted themselves into places and times where they were not present, constructed pyramids they never saw, and taken credit for Afrikan civilizations that are definitively located in Afrika. Ashkenazi and Sephardic Jews credit themselves with building civilization in Kemet and the Sudan while having built nothing in Turkey (Sephardic home in Eurasia) or Khazaria/Ashkenaz (Ashkenazi home in Eurasia) during or before this time in history.

Being the first people on the planet and the founders of civilization holds tremendous racial weight and relevance—particularly when it is known and acknowledged. Unfortunately, it holds the same weight if people falsely believe these things about you and your group. Jews have strategically placed themselves into the shoes of the Black founders of civilization. They have done this in two major ways:

1) Being the first people on the planet simply means there is no Earthly mother or father to Black people. Out of our DNA code comes all other peoples on this planet. This is science. But it also holds spiritual and religious value because it means the only people who can credibly claim to have been created by God are Black people. Everyone else genetically derives from our DNA. This is a scientific fact. But it is also a spiritual fact. It does not mean we are incapable of being outperformed, as our condition in 2022 exemplifies. However, our performance does not change the fact Black people are by definition God's Chosen People. Like Adam

and Eve, we are the only people "God made." Everyone else came from us going forth and multiplying. This reality naturally holds spiritual weight and status for any member of the Afrikan family.

Jews simply ignore this reality and claim themselves, through biblical interpretation and allegory, to be God's Chosen People. And for those who do not know who they are and what they are doing, which is most people, it works.

2) Black people have been cast as subhuman through Jewish biblical interpretation. Our image as a race has been sullied throughout the planet. Our history has been systematically suppressed on every continent, even Afrika. Our great leaders have been targeted for international extermination.

Our culture is under constant attack worldwide. Our identities have been confused through integration, religious conquest, and NWO "humanism" indoctrination. Unfortunately, in many ways, we are beginning to become the living examples of horrible ideas originally formulated in the Jewish mind.

At the Council of Jamnia in A.D. 90, which Jews claim took place in modern-day Israel, the Jewish rabbis concocted a biblical myth designed to lay the pretext for the subjugation of Black people for centuries to come. This pornographic, homophilic myth is commonly referred to as the "Hamitic Myth." It became part of the Babylonian Talmud and later had a version inserted into the Holy Bible:

> Now I cannot beget the fourth son whose children I would have ordered to serve you and your brothers: Therefore it must be Canaan, your first born, whom they enslave. And since you have disabled me . . . doing the ugly things [raping me] in the blackness of night, Canaan's children shall be born ugly and black; Moreover, because you twisted your head around to see my nakedness, your grandchildren's hair shall be twisted into kinks; and their eyes red; again because you jested at my misfortune, theirs shall swell; and because you neglected my nakedness, they shall go naked, and their male members [penises] shall go shamefully elongated: Men of this race are called Negroes, their forefather Canaan commanded them to love theft and fornication, to be

> banded together in hatred of their masters and never to tell the truth.
>
> —Talmud, chapter 9, vv. 25-7

This is the foundational historic basis for misclassifying Black people as inferior. It is 100% of Jewish design, and it is based in Jewish long-term interests which have nothing to do with truth. In fact, it totally subjugates the truth of ancient history to cause God's Chosen People and the founders of civilization to be reviled by all groups as a product of God's judgement for homosexual rape of our own fathers. This is Babylonian Talmudic behavior we had nothing to do with creating.

In has been argued the Jewish Hamitic Myth marks the origin of the modern concept of "racism." Before this, conflict was based in land, power, resources, empire, etc. It was never based on the idea that one group of people was inherently inferior based on their pigment and genetic composition. The Jew created the concept of racism almost 2,000 years ago, to the detriment of Black people. We owe them quite a debt.

This strategic combination has landed wonders for the Jews. As the writers of many of the earliest Eurasiatic religious texts and posing as the falsely perceived God's Chosen People, Jews have directly or indirectly incorporated their negative Jewish ideas about Black people into the religious literature of most groups. They simply insert their desired lies into these translations of biblical texts and watch their poison penetrate and spread. Even when we examine the Mormon religion, they have a racist story about the origin of Black people.

The Hamitic Myth was part of the justification for the Transatlantic Slave Trade. As discussed earlier, it was the Jews who conceived, started, architected, and profited most from Black enslavement since the 1600s. It was the creation of the Hamitic Myth and centuries of nurturing those ideas about Black "inferiority" that made chattel slavery feasible in America.

While Jews were busy subjecting our reputation to slander, they were practicing a perverted religious system with a sexually perverse Satanic religious text: the Babylonian Talmud. The Talmud promotes homosexuality, pedophilia, bestiality, theft, murder, lying, cheating, stealing, and other psychopathic behavior. Yet, they present themselves as God's Chosen People.

The Other Israel
archive.org/details/theotherisraelhd

One of the interesting things about Jews claiming to be God's Chosen People is their almost complete absence of forgiveness. They committed treason against the nation of Germany in WWI and created the conditions that led to World War II (WWII). The Germans accepted their declaration of war and resisted. WWII ended in 1945. It has been nearly 80 years! Jews are still collecting money and still have not forgiven any Germans for a war Jews started. That is not what we would expect from God's Chosen People. Yet, they are on the front lines denying Black peoples' rights to reparations for slavery that they were inextricably involved in. According to the Jewish narrative, our grandparents fought to get the Jews out of the gas chambers, but Jews fought to keep Black people enslaved. Additionally, Jews receive funds from America for the "Holocaust" Americans saved them from in Germany, yet Jews fight to deny Black people reparations for chattel slavery that happened here in America. It seems to me that since Americans saved Jews from the Holocaust, **JEWS OWE AMERICA**. Why is America paying Jews for saving them?!

Our very identity as the origin of the concept of God's Chosen People has been stolen by the Jews. Our identity as the mothers and fathers of civilization has been hidden and slandered by the Jews. Even their claim to the religion of Judaism gives them an undeserved place in the minds of most Christians as the fathers of the so-called "Judeo-Christian" faith. This is simply more identity theft.

The oldest creation story in the history of the world is the Asar, Aset, and Heru story from Kemet. The Greek names are Osiris, Isis, and Horus. This was the first story of an immaculately conceived savior. This and other similar Trinity stories from Kemet are the foundation for most of the spiritual principles and religions practiced around the world. The Christian Trinity is based on this story. The only major change to the Trinity construct is that Aset (originally adopted as "Mary—Mother or God") was eventually replaced by the Holy Ghost. The idea of a savior, made in the image and likeness of his father, God—who comes to redeem civilization from the clutches of wickedness—is consistent. Another difference is Jesus came as the Prince of Peace, and Heru came as a warrior to defeat his evil Uncle Seth.

When it is all said and done, the idea there is a spirit inside of us that can rise through adversity and conquer the evil in this world with the help of the Creator, is consistent from ancient Kemet in 2000 B.C. through Christianity today. Islam calls for strength through Allah via the Prophet Muhammad, and Judaism calls for strength through Yahweh via the rabbi.

The interesting thing about the Jews of today is they have taken our ancient story and perverted it significantly. They replaced the savior Heru with themselves as God's Chosen People; but they have no responsibility to save or help anyone other than Jews. There are no saviors in their story. Jesus is not the Son of God in the Babylonian Talmud. The Talmud refers to Mary as a harlot and curses Jesus to burn in boiling hot excrement. Jews, and Jews alone, are considered the children of God. Everyone else is equal to the value of animals and exist to be their servants. This is a transition from the Afrikan principle of being King. A *Suten* in Afrika was often seen as having a direct link to the Creator. And the people were all looked at as servants to the King. The *Suten* was supposed to love his people and serve the interests of the nation. A good *Suten* was known for these qualities along with his capacity to govern and protect the kingdom. Jews of the Babylonian Talmudic type do not view their relationship with God as giving them responsibility to help others; rather they view it as a responsibility to abuse, rob, cheat, and kill others.

More Jewish theft can be discovered in the layout of Washington, D.C. Benjamin Banneker remembered the plans by heart for the layout of the nation's capital after Pierre Charles L'Enfant abruptly left with them. The layout was clearly based on Kemetic elements. The most obvious example is the Washington Monument. The monument actually represents resurrection. In the ancient story of Asar, he was murdered by his evil twin brother Seth, who gathered 24 conspirators, murdered Asar, cut his body into 14 pieces, and spread them throughout the Nile Valley of Kemet. When his wife discovered Asar's death, Aset combed the land gathering the parts of his body. She found all the pieces except for his phallus.

She put his body back together and wrapped him in white loincloth for burial. He was so overjoyed at her loyalty and commitment to him even in his death, that he impregnated her with a child. Because there was no physical intimacy between the two, it was an immaculate conception. It represented Asar pouring his wisdom, knowledge, character, strength, courage, sight, tenacity, intelligence, honesty, integrity, truth, etc., into a seed she would bring forth into life. The message was that if a man picks a good woman, she can duplicate him even in his absence, because she will spread the best of him into future generations.

Since Asar was able to spiritually impregnate his wife in physical death, the *tekhenu*, or obelisk, was resurrected in his memory. It represents his erect phallus with the capacity to implant the seed of life into the world. This is what the Washington Monument represents. It is Asar's power to resurrect life. It is Asar's phallus. It is not pornographic. It is spiritual. It means life.

Jews not only hide our history and pervert the spiritual meanings and interpretations of Afrikan culture and spirituality, but they also pervert our symbols. In ancient Kemet, there is a popular symbol representing spiritual sight or the third eye. This represents discernment and the ability to see the invisible world of ideas, thoughts, feelings, future, etc. It is called the "All-Seeing Eye of Heru."

The Savior Heru lost an eye in battle while avenging his father's death at the hands of his evil Uncle Seth. Though he lost his physical eye in battle, he tuned into his spiritual eye of discernment and went on to defeat his uncle, ascend to the throne, and restore the kingdom to balance and harmony. This symbol represents spiritual sight, insight, discernment, and wisdom.

We remember the Jews claiming their control over the U.S. secret societies and their ideologies from Protocol No. XI:

> **This constituted a base for our organization of** *secret masonry which is not known to and whose aims are not even suspected by these cattle, the Goys. They have been decoyed by us into our numerous ostensible organizations, which appear to be Masonic lodges, so as to divert the attention of their coreligionists.*

Eye of Heru

Since the Jews already told us as early as 1903 that they control all of the secret societies, it would be overkill for me to use this space to prove it. Instead, I will show how they use the theft of Afrikan history and spiritual tradition to push their agenda. Let us look at the back of the dollar bill.

We remember the Jews took control over the American economy in 1913 with the creation of the Federal Reserve. In 1935, dollars began to be printed with a pyramid and a version of the Eye of Heru on the back. The pyramids come from Kemet in Afrika and the Eye of Heru symbol comes from Kemet in Afrika. The obvious question is, "What are they doing on American money?"

The answer is as obvious as the question: identity theft. The Jews are showing their mastery and "sight" over the most powerful currency in the world. They stole the knowledge and wisdom of the builders of civilization (Black people), used our physical labor to build the Republic (chattel slavery), stole the American Republic from the Anglo-Saxons through financial tyranny (Federal Reserve), and are using this power to dominate the planet. And only they have the insight to see what is going on. The rays of the Sun shining around the Eye of Heru knockoff represents God watching over them. In other words, they are God's Chosen People.

If one talks to an Anglo-Saxon or Black Mason, they will say this explanation is ridiculous. They will repeat whatever explanation was given to them by the head of their lodge or remark they can never share the secrets of the craft. The secret of the craft is the Jews control the money and are exterminating the non-Jews on planet Earth. The secret is they stole the identity of the people who built civilization, used Anglo-Saxon muscle to wreak international dominion and havoc over the Black world, and are about to exterminate their ancient adversaries: White folks.

What is amazing is that Christians have all of this information available to them in their Bibles written by the Jews. Even though the Jews incorporated their own perverse fables and changes according to their designs, they copied most of these texts from sources that originated in Afrikan spirituality. So much of the truth about Afrikan history is plainly stated in the King James Bible text.

For instance:

"Yet I am the LORD thy God from the land of Egypt, and thou shalt know no god but me: for there is no saviour beside me." (Hosea 13:4)
Translation: God is from Afrika or Spirituality is from Afrika.

"To the only wise God our Saviour, be glory and majesty, dominion and power, both now and ever. Amen." (Jude 1:25)
Translation: God's true name is Amen.

"And blessed be his glorious name for ever: and let the whole earth be filled with his glory; Amen, and Amen." (Psalms 72:19)
Translation: God's true name is Amen.

"Now unto the King eternal, immortal, invisible, the only wise God, be honour and glory for ever and ever. Amen." (1 Timothy 1:17)
Translation: God's true name is Amen.

"Who only hath immortality, dwelling in the light which no man can approach unto; whom no man hath seen, nor can see: to whom be honour and power everlasting. Amen." (1 Timothy 6:16)
Translation: God's true name is Amen.

The Holy Bible, in countless verses throughout, instructs believers to refer to God as Amen. He is the only savior and only true and wise God. Amen was the name for God during the 18th Dynastic Period under the rulership of Neb Pehty Ra Ahmose, who expelled the Hyksos invaders from Kemet with the rallying cry of "Never Again." He was expressing that never again would the great kingdoms of Kemet fall asleep enough for Asiatic invaders to come in and oppress our people. Have we heard that cry anywhere else?

In this same 18th Dynasty, the most feared ruler in the history of the world became *Suten*. His name was Menkhepera Tehudimes (aka Thutmose III). He worshipped the Black God Amen and ruled around 1479 B.C, nearly 3,500 years ago. He led his armies in campaigns that are still recalled through our language today. His first battle was in a city called Megiddo. He left the city is such disarray the people who witnessed the aftermath of the battle claimed, "The end of the world will look like this." This is where the term "Armageddon" is derived.

As the great ruler continued his battles, he began the process of bringing the captured leaders of defeated nations back to Kemet for indoctrination into the worship of the Black God Amen. This indoctrination was so thorough the effects are still being felt 3,500 years later. We just saw the Bible verses instructing Christians to refer to God as Amen. We also see every religion ends its prayers with "Amen." In Christian churches, the dominant affirmation is,

"Amen." This stems from systematic indoctrination of foreign nationals with the worship of the God Amen from 3,500 years in the past.

Many Black people comment on the indoctrination we have received into worshipping Islam, Judaism, and Christianity; but few of us know that we actually started this process. It was for a different reason. Menkhepera Tehudimes was working to ensure no nations would ever again reign terror on Kemet. He surmised that by indoctrinating them into the worship of Amen, it would prevent them from wanting to destroy Amen's people. He may not have absolutely accomplished this. However, he certainly made an indelible mark on religion and spirituality that is visible to those with sight today.

If we understand Jews are at the head of all Masonry, whether they are seen or not, we will understand the early history of America better. For instance, the name "America" itself derives from Kemet. It is literally Amen (God) + Ra (God) + Ka (Spirit). If one drops the "n" in "Amen," changes the "a" to "i," and changes the "K" to "c," we walk away with Ame + ri + ca.

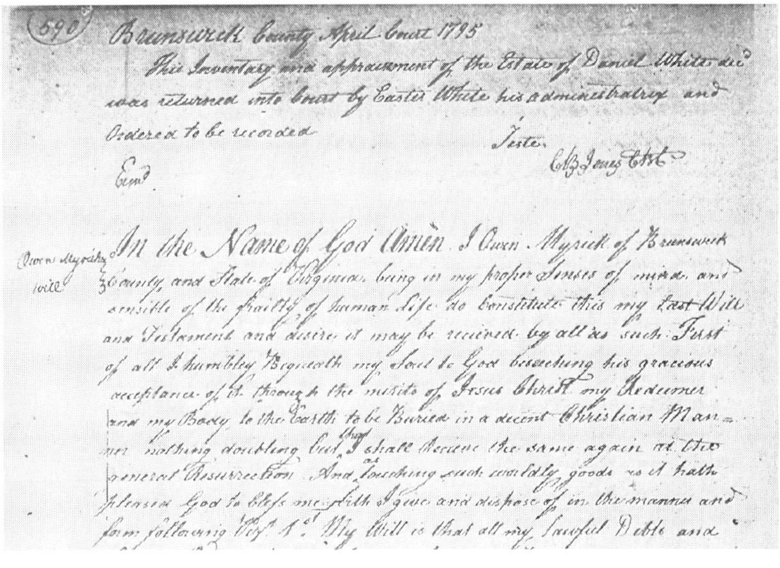
590

Brunswick County April Court 1795

This Inventory and appraisement of the Estate of Daniel White dec'd was returned into Court by Easter White his administratrix and Ordered to be recorded

Teste

[illegible] Jones Clk

Exd

Owen Myrick's will

In the Name of God Amen I Owen Myrick of Brunswick County and State of Virginia being in my proper Senses of mind and sensible of the frailty of human Life do Constitute this my Last Will and Testament and desire it may be received by all as such First of all I humbley Bequeath my Soul to God beseeching his gracious acceptance of it through the merits of Jesus Christ my Redeemer and my Body to the Earth to be Buried in a decent Christian Manner nothing doubting but I shall Receive the same again at the general Resurrection And touching such worldly goods as it hath pleased God to bless me with I give and dispose of in the manner and form following Viz. 1st My Will is that all my Lawful Debts and

Owen Myrick's last will and testament, the author's personal family's historical freedom from slavery

This country was not only built on the physical blood, sweat, and tears of Afrikan people, but the very name of the country comes from our ancestral spirituality. And the Jews know it because they are the ones who did this. Even the early Founding Fathers—like George Washington, who was a Mason—showed their worship of the God Amen:

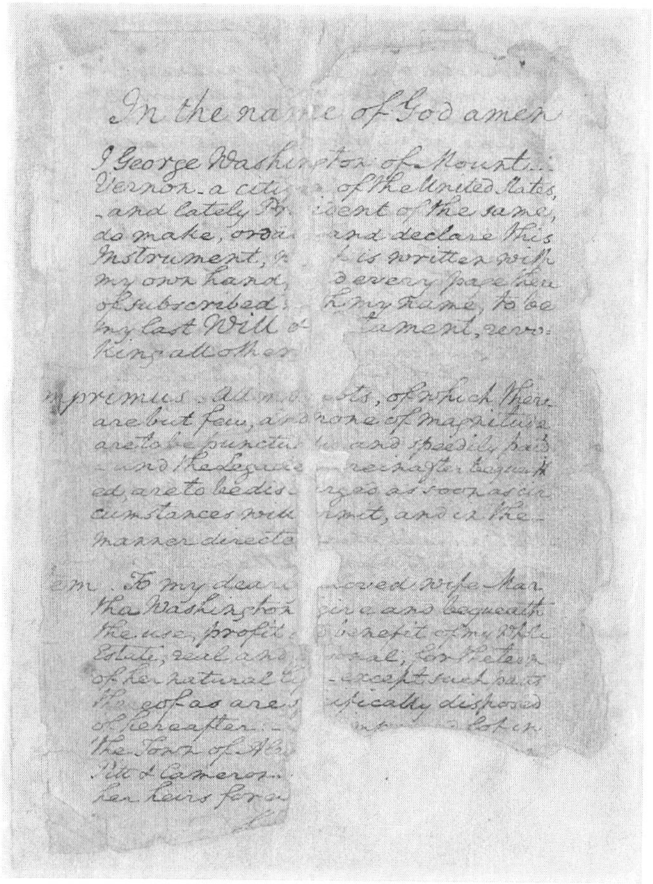
In the name of God amen

I George Washington of Mount Vernon a citi of the United States, and lately Pr ident of the same, do make, ord and declare this Instrument, is written with my own hand, every page there of subscribed h my name, to be my last Will of tament, revo king all other

One page of George Washington's last will and testament

As we can see, it was common during the 1700s and 1800s for White slave owners in America to refer to God as Amen in their last will and testaments. Of course, many of them were Masons. And many of them were Jews. The important thing to recognize is they are all referring to God in the name used by our Afrikan Ancestors 3,500 years ago, and they are all following the direction of the Bible in calling God by his rightful name according to scripture. But the Jews keep this public information hidden and censored in plain sight.

After seeing this type of obvious truth, it would be a bit much for the average White man or woman to digest. In many cases, it would mean they have been tricked into believing the very people they built their country based off of are cursed by God to be in a subservient condition. But many would probably appreciate learning the hard truth simply because it is undeniable, obvious, overt truth. At the end of the day, they still control civilization in the modern age.

Jews would be mortified. It would completely strip them of any cover for the genocide they are inflicting on the world. In particular, Anglo-Saxons would shed any sympathy, compassion, or respect for Jews being God's Chosen People, and instead classify them as the obvious psychopaths they have proven themselves to be. The shift of White Anglo-Saxon aggression away from Black people onto the true oppressors of the planet might be enough for Black people to wake up as well. Once everyone is viewing the lies the Jews tell in order to keep us preoccupied fighting one another while they kill us all, we will all look at them for who and what they are.

They are actually what Jesus Christ classified them as in the Holy Bible:

"Ye are of your father the devil, and the lusts of your father ye will do. He was a murderer from the beginning, and abode not in the truth, because there is no truth in him. When he speaketh a lie, he speaketh of his own: for he is a liar, and the father of it." (John 8:44)

"I know thy works, and tribulation, and poverty, (but thou art rich) and I know the blasphemy of them which say they are Jews, and are not, but are the synagogue of Satan." (Revelation 2:9)

"Behold, I will make them of the synagogue of Satan, which say they are Jews, and are not, but do lie; behold, I will make them to come and worship before thy feet, and to know that I have loved thee." (Revelation 3:9)

They are not God's Chosen People. They are not victims. **And as Jesus stated, they are not even Jews.** So, from this point forward, we will no longer classify them by that name and continue insulting the true people of the book. Instead, we will collectively call the Ashkenazim and Sephardim "Bolsheviks." It is historical. It is appropriate. It is timely. And it is foreshadowing. Once we study the Bolshevik Revolution, we will all understand what the planet is facing now that they have control of the U.S. Republic and are trying to launch a war with Russia.

BOLSHEVIKS ARE THE PROBLEM!

FAUCI KILLS

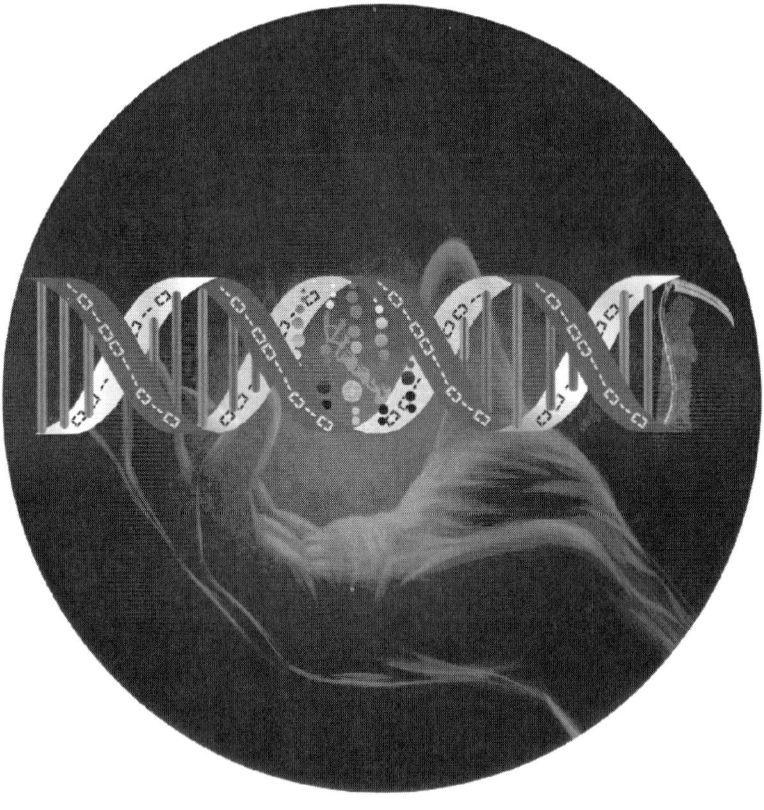

"WE WILL NEVER FORGET!"

5

COVID-19: THE ~~JEWISH~~ BOLSHEVIK GLOBAL EXTERMINATION CAMPAIGN

The 21st century Bolsheviks have come to kill us all. And they have intentionally left their mark on it for all of us with a third eye (discernment) to see. Let us talk about The Fauci.

To begin, Anthony Fauci and Bill Gates are two of the faces of the global pandemic. Of course, they are both Anglo-Saxon. However, this slavery-to-genocide initiative is being architected in the mind of one central body: the Bolsheviks.

A reasonable starting point to discuss this genocidal initiative in modern times would be with Henry Kissinger, Bolshevik author of the National Security Study Memorandum 200: Implications of Worldwide Population Growth for U.S. Security and Overseas Interests (NSSM200), also known as the "Kissinger Report," completed on Tuesday, December 10, 1974. In it, Kissinger laid the foundation for justifying the extermination of the world's population. He focused on "controlling" the populations of Third World countries, meaning Afrika and parts of Asia. Because it focused on killing Black people and other non-Whites, it was well received by U.S. President Gerald Ford and became an integral part of U.S. foreign policy. Under COINTELPRO—a counterintelligence program run by J. Edgar Hoover focused on killing and subduing the Black Panther Party—the Federal Bureau of Investigation practiced genocide on Black people in America. NSSM 200 gave the Bolsheviks an opportunity to focus White Anglo-Saxon attention on exterminating Black people and other non-Whites the world over.

The Bolsheviks used the resources and muscle of White America to create the system of genocide that would later be used to exterminate Anglo-Saxons worldwide. However, before the system could be used against White Americans and other Whites around the world, the Bolsheviks convinced White Americans to build, maintain, expand, and refine the process of killing Black people around the world. If President Ford or any of the White Americans in politics in the 1970s had understood NSSM 200 was a program designed to create a system for their ultimate extermination, they would never have agreed to this type of suicide. However, since it was sold as a program to exterminate Black people abroad, it became U.S. foreign policy.

By 1981, a deadly condition called Gay Related Immune Deficiency or Gay Related Infectious Diseases (GRID) stormed America. In 1982 the name was changed to Acquired Immune Deficiency Syndrome (AIDS). This deadly disease sent shock waves through the entire world. The condition was actually a description of what was happening to the LGBT community. They were reportedly having thousands of sex partners, passing diseases, partying incessantly, and injecting poisons/toxins into their bodies through continuous drug abuse. This combination of factors was destroying their immune systems, leading to death via deadly forms of cancer and other diseases.

Around the same time AIDS emerged, Afrikans in the Congo were dying from an experimental polio vaccine that was given to over 1 million of them in 1958 by Dr. Hilary Koprowski, a Bolshevik doctor. By the 1980s, this polio vaccine was killing vast numbers of our Brothers and Sisters who had received those injections.

These two realities provided the perfect pretext for the Bolsheviks to launch their international global genocide campaign. First, they blamed Afrikan people for having sex with monkeys and creating the AIDS virus. This removed any discussion about the vaccine that had an estimated 25-year incubation period before it killed our people. Koprowski's germ warfare was totally removed from the narrative. Secondly, they renamed GRID to AIDS in order to remove the stigma of the cultural behavior that was creating the deaths in America: homophilia. They claimed Black people having sex with monkeys in Afrika brought AIDS to America and spread it to the LGBT community.

Now the Bolsheviks had successfully created a narrative that hid two realities they became keenly aware of:

1) Bolshevik-produced vaccines can be administered to kill people with a short-or long-term death incubation period.
2) The LGBT culture of uninhibited perverse sexuality, coupled with not resting the body and *injecting the body with poisonous toxins*, can destroy people's immune systems and kill them.

This was fantastic for the Bolsheviks. They could simply choose to hide the truth about these two death sentences from the people. Instead of discouraging these behaviors, they would promote them to the world as "The Way." *Take Vaccinations* and *Be Gay* became their agendas for global extermination. Either of these practices or a combination of the two can kill the healthiest person. This became the constant push on the world population over the next 40 years. Movies, science, math, documentaries, investments, education—you name it, it is in there. We call it "the Fag or the Jab" or "Operation Serpent & the Rainbow."

To facilitate ensuring their death agenda, they added one final feature to this genocide machine. Dr. Anthony Fauci, head of the National Institute of Allergy and Infectious Diseases (NIAID) by 1984, prescribed a lethal drug called AZT to all AIDS patients. (Special thanks to Dr. Bryan Ardis for his research on the snake venom aspect of the pandemic. Without his work, we would never have thought to investigate to see if AZT was related to snake venom. Now we know it might be. Hence, Operation Serpent & the Rainbow.) In short, Fauci took patients whose behavior was destroying their immune systems, and instead of encouraging them to live a healthier lifestyle and work to build their natural immunity, he prescribed them AZT, the death potion to finish them.

It later became known more people died from AZT than AIDS. It is pretty much common knowledge today. But few people know it was Fauci who was in charge of prescribing this lethal poison. Interestingly, "Fauci" is an Italian name that means "sickle," like the type commonly depicted with the Grim Reaper.

Dr. Anthony Fauci

This father of death has been a proxy in the Bolshevik war against the world's population for quite some time. Fauci is a real-life Grim Reaper who preys on the naivete of innocent men, women, and children of all races. It appears his appetite for death and destruction is insatiable.

Operation Serpent & the Rainbow is the perfect segue into the discussion about The Fauci. Since January 2020, when America was informed about the new outbreak, there have been two primary social concerns troubling American people: The Fauci and the transgender LGBT nonsense in our schools. These two issues continuously rear their heads and have led to many demonstrations and much resistance around the country. What we haven't surmised is that this is not new, but it is an accelerated version of the AIDS construct. This is how it was done.

Based on Dr. Ardis's research, we believe U.S. scientists developed a snake venom-based bioweapon that can be transmitted by multiple means. Snake venom may be the primary ingredient in the "spike protein," which is also laced with HIV. We have more than adequate information to confirm Fauci used his position as head of NIAID to fund GoFR. Gain-of-function research simply means scientists take an organism like a virus or bacteria that is otherwise harmless to humans, and through scientific manipulation turn it into a harmful bioweapon that can infect, harm, and/or kill people. It is a specialized field of biochemical warfare. Fauci funded research to study how to take the coronavirus from a bat, make it more harmful, and transmit it to people. The only logical purpose for this research was to produce a bioweapon to unleash on the public.

Based on the multitude of patents for the improperly labeled "COVID-19 vaccinations" that existed long before 2020, we are convinced the objective for releasing The Fauci bioweapon called COVID-19 on the public was to convince everyone to take the COVID-19 "vaccinations." These harmful injections are a more virulent form of the snake venom-based bioweapon released at the end of 2019. In other words, they created the COVID-19 "vaccinations" first in order to poison the world's population with a snake venom-based bioweapon that will not only poison us, but can also rewrite our DNA to produce a snake venom-based bioweapon from within our own bodies. It was always the goal to invade our genome and integrate it with animal DNA and AI. This process is called transhumanism. This is why doctors and scientists who have studied these injections have found all sorts of parasites, metallic substances, circuitry, nanobots (microscopic robots), and other substances inside of these injections. They are 21st century bioweapon technology designed to invade our DNA and turn our bodies into communication devices that can be accessed remotely via the Internet. This technology is called messenger ribonucleic acid (mRNA). In short, these bioweapons are designed to either:

1) Kill us
2) Significantly harm us
3) Transition us from people into part person, part animal, part machine

4) Turn us into receivers for remote access and control by the architects of this design

Dr. David Martin on Calculated Injection Genocide
rumble.com/vk2bya-exclusive-dr.-david-martin-just-ended-covid-fauci-doj-politicians-in-one-in.html

As bizarre as this sounds, there is more evidence to prove this is true than there is to debunk it as conspiracy theory. In the years to come, this reality will become common knowledge.

Dr. Ariyana Love on Israeli Ownership of Injection Patent Technology
rumble.com/vqhjbo-doctor-dead-after-vaxx-discovery-dr.-noack-dead-after-locating-graphene-hyd.html

In preparation for this genocide program on the world population, the Bill & Melinda Gates Foundation, Johns Hopkins University, and the WEF headed by Klaus Schwab, held a public dry run in New York City on October 18, 2019. It was called Event 201: A Global Pandemic Exercise. They discussed how they would respond to a major international "novel" coronavirus outbreak. They publicly strategized using "soft power" to assist in the censorship of Americans who spread "misinformation." From page 39 of the book *The Truth About COVID-19: Exposing the Great Reset, Lockdowns, Vaccine Passports, and the New Normal* by Dr. Joseph Mercola and Ronnie Cummins, we get:

Event 201 Predicted "Need" for Censorship

> Event 201 planners spent a great deal of time discussing ways to limit and counter the spread of expected "misinformation" about the pandemic and subsequent vaccines. In addition to outright censoring certain views, Event 201 introduced a plan that included the use of "soft power," a term referring to stealth influencing. This strategy uses celebrities and other social media influencers to model ideal behavior and promote adherence to pandemic response edicts.

Event 201

youtube.com/watch?v=Vm1-DnxRiPM

After publicly participating in this dry run for world genocide, each of the players took their positions in pushing the Bolshevik agenda. The audacity of people to publicly practice launching an international pandemic in front of the world, film it, and make the video available for public viewing, represents the mind of an incorrigible creature. The brilliance of it is the major players we see are mostly non-Bolsheviks. So even if people figure out what they did and decide to bring them to justice, we will only be targeting the proxies, not the Bolsheviks themselves.

Roughly 10 weeks after Event 201, the genocide plan was unleashed. The spread of a "novel" coronavirus was reported. The virus was said to be very contagious and lethal. The MSM began to report massive deaths in the U.S. and around the world by April 2020. The Fauci became the talk of the world, and Phase 1 of the implementation began.

To be clear, there is confusion about whether the initial sickness came from a virus or a bioweapon. Based on Dr. Ardis's new findings, I surmise it was a combination of both. The etymology of the word virus is "venom" or "poisonous secretion." Since we now believe the spike protein has a snake-venom base and was engineered in a lab through GoFR, we also believe it is both a virus (venom or poisonous secretion) and a bioweapon since it was engineered to be delivered to people as a solid, liquid, or gas. It is not natural since it was created in a lab, but it relies on the properties of a natural poison: snake venom. We believe it can travel through the air like a virus, through water or injections like a liquid, or pills and food as a solid. The most dangerous delivery of this venom is through injections, because they can add any number of other harmful ingredients to the cocktail and go directly into the bloodstream.

Dr. Bryan Ardis Watch the Water

rumble.com/v10mnew-live-world-premiere-watch-the-water.html

Also, we believe GoFR funded by Fauci and the NIAID engineered a way to deliver spike protein to people using a bat coronavirus as a transportation system. In other words, we believe they created a way to take a harmless bat virus, load it with a dangerous lab-made snake venom, and deliver the toxin into people through the air. We also believe they can deliver the poison through liquid or gas. This mix of transportation methods makes it difficult for scientists and/or doctors to understand what is actually happening.

After unleashing the initial bioweapon, the next phase of their plan was to kill as many people as possible to scare the public into longing for a solution. The solution provided by the Bolsheviks was to condition the public for their primary objective: the bioweapon injection. Gates and Fauci almost immediately began discussing having a "vaccine" ready for release to the public within one year. This was "genocide grooming."

Next, the Bolsheviks used their power in the hospitals to ensure infected people would not get appropriate treatment for the bioweapon. Rather, people were rushed to ventilators where they were murdered. It is important to note that an incentive structure for hospitals was implemented that made COVID-19-labeled deaths quite profitable. It quickly became far more lucrative for hospitals to allow people to die, or kill people in the hospital, than to save their lives.

When U.S. President Donald Trump suggested Americans use hydroxychloroquine (HCQ), he almost destroyed their entire genocide program. However, he did not use his power as commander-in-chief to enforce this suggestion. As a consequence, the genocide continued.

By May 2020, it became increasingly important to control the information narrative and classify every cold, flu, or similar sickness as The Fauci. In this way, they could get people acclimated to taking PCR tests that have nothing to do with determining sickness. These tests were used as a tool to classify people as testing positive for The Fauci so they could put them through the hospital protocol and kill them. It was also a way to train us out of intellectual decision making and discernment. Never before had we routinely tested healthy people to see if we were sick. This is impractical and rather ridiculous. When we feel sick, we are probably sick. Otherwise, we are OK. In this new reality, we had to check every week or every few days for sickness we do not possess. Once conditioned into this behavior, the Bolsheviks are able to simply change the sensitivity of the PCR kits and classify more people as testing positive for The Fauci. This process allows the pandemic to be never-ending.

We are now convinced PCR kits are nefarious. Our understanding is they are used for the transfection of DNA between animals in the cloning process. They may be a means to transfect DNA from one source into everyone who swabs with it: transhumanism.

After the Bolsheviks stole the 2020 election from Trump, the road to massive genocide was open and clear. This is the implementation phase that drove the release of the original bioweapon in 2019. By December 2020, they began bioweapon injections. These injections spread throughout the planet. Americans were initially informed we would get one "vaccination" and become immune to The Fauci. Instead, the Western Israeli government has been pressuring U.S. citizens to receive ongoing bioweapon injections. Millions worldwide have either been harmfully affected or killed by this bioweapon;

yet the Bolsheviks are now pushing it on babies, at birth in some places.

One of the most disturbing aspects of the injection genocide phase has been the hospitals' role in the process of premeditated murder. By the time the injections were deployed, Fauci as head of NIAID, authorized one medication to be prescribed to patients who tested positive for The Fauci: remdesivir, a drug (snake venom-based, according to Dr. Ardis) known to kill patients as recently as 2019. In fact, Fauci quoted a 2019 study of an Ebola trial on Afrikan people where doctors were instructed to stop administering remdesivir because it killed over 50% of the patients *and* it didn't work. He oversaw the trial as head of NIAID, so we know he knows remdesivir destroys body organs. *He quoted the 2019 trial study that proved it!* Yet he used the same study to justify administering this potentially snake venom-based drug to The Fauci patients. As head of NIAID, Fauci only authorized hospitals in this country one approved treatment for The Fauci: remdesivir.

Dr. Peterson Pierre Explains the Process for Murder by Remdesivir
bitchute.com/video/KQ8XpSsfbxVC

As stated earlier, remdesivir destroys the kidneys. When a patient tests positive in a hospital for The Fauci, they are often administered remdesivir. Once remdesivir causes the kidneys to malfunction, liquid backs up into the lungs of the patient and they begin to have problems breathing. The hospital rams a ventilator in or down their throat. A few days later, they are dead. This happens every single day all across this country and most people do not have any idea this is premeditated murder. It is also murder-for-hire because the hospitals and some of the doctors get paid handsomely to facilitate this process.

So, whether from The Fauci injections or remdesivir, people are potentially having snake venom shoved into their systems. They are most certainly being murdered. And this organized poisoning of American citizens is perfectly in accordance with the instructions set forth in *The Protocols of the Learned Elders of Zion*.

Let's remember Protocol No. X:

> . . . **it is necessary continuously to disturb the relationship between the people and the government in all countries, and so to exhaust everybody by the dissension, hostility, struggle, hatred, and even martyrdom, hunger, inoculation of diseases, and misery, and to make the Goys see no other solution than an appeal to our money and complete rule.**

The Bolsheviks found a means through this sadistic process of torture and murder to put the world's population on a conveyor belt for genocide. Native Americans, Europeans, Black people, and more groups have been specifically targeted by these bioweapons. But there is one particular group of interest who is not as susceptible to getting sick from this bioweapon as the rest of us. According to a July 15, 2020 *BMC Medicine* article entitled, "New insights into genetic susceptibility of COVID-19: an *ACE2* and *TMPRSS2* polymorphism analysis":

> . . . Coronavirus Disease 2019 (COVID-19), caused by the severe acute respiratory syndrome coronavirus 2 (SARS-CoV-2), has now been confirmed worldwide. Yet, COVID-19 is strangely and tragically selective . . .
>
> . . . We found that the distribution of deleterious variants in *ACE2* differs among 9 populations in gnomAD (v3). Specifically, 39% (24/61) and 54% (33/61) of deleterious variants in ACE2 occur in African/African-American and Non-Finnish European populations, respectively. Prevalence of deleterious variants among Latino/Admixed American, East Asian, Finnish, and South Asian populations is 2-10%, while Amish and **Ashkenazi Jewish populations do not appear to carry such variants in ACE2 coding regions.** [Emphasis added]

BMC Medicine Article on Susceptibility to COVID-19
bmcmedicine.biomedcentral.com/articles/10.1186/s12916-020-01673-z

By now, it should come as no surprise the Bolsheviks appear to have some strange level of immunity to The Fauci. The fact Bolsheviks make up an unusually high percentage of the scientists involved in the creation of chemical/biological weapons should not shock us either. The Fauci is a well-thought-out biowarfare genocide attack on the people of the planet. It is being executed with great efficiency and success.

Dr. Ariyana Love Speaks on Bolshevik Creation of Ethnic-Based Bioweapons
rumble.com/vz7rd3-dna-under-siege-bioweapons-developed-in-ukraine-specifically-target-abraham.html

Fauci wins $1 million Israeli prize for 'defending science'
apnews.com/article/joe-biden-donald-trump-science-pandemics-israel-25c3a68083ce77652a4330e944cced73

At this point, we should be clear on the genocide aspect of this Bolshevik bioweapon assault. However, we also have to examine the slavery aspect. More than anything else in history, the Bolsheviks have been enslavers. This is why we do not separate the Sephardim from the Ashkenazim in our analysis of the Bolsheviks. Many Whites separate them, but the originators of the Hamitic Myth, financiers and organizers of the Transatlantic Slave Trade, and the second-in-command of the Confederacy were all Sephardic. So, from a Black perspective, we see the Sephardim being at least as bad historically as the Ashkenazim.

The enslavement aspect of this assault is possibly more terrifying than the killing aspect. In order to put this into proper context, **IT IS ABSOLUTELY NECESSARY TO WATCH THE FOLLOWING VIDEO.** It provides the military science and context for us to understand what they have the technology and capability to do scientifically; and it shows their stated intentions. Further, this video was uploaded to YouTube in 2018, before this slavery-to-genocide war was unleashed.

Charles A. Morgan on 21st Century Warfare at
U.S. Military Academy West Point
bitchute.com/video/iQF3dJk5HBmY

The information in this video is extremely concerning for anyone who understands what mRNA technology is designed to do. It is designed to enter the DNA code of people and change it. These changes are designed to be irreversible and pass down generation to generation through our new DNA sequences. Essentially, whatever changes occur to our DNA code are intended to be permanent.

These mRNA injections are designed to add instructions to our DNA code to produce "spike protein." At this point, we know spike protein is a bioweapon that destroys organs, creates blood clots, and destroys natural immune systems. We strongly believe the core ingredient in spike protein is some scientifically processed form of snake venom. Therefore, what is actually happening is people are being injected with a bioweapon that makes their body become a manufacturing plant for snake venom (spike protein). In some weird way, they are turning people into walking serpents.

Dr. Bryan Ardis Discussing Snake Venom & The Fauci
brighteon.com/3d7a771d-b4bb-45b8-beea-6fed78d21e98

If this is not bad enough, we now have clear evidence all of these injections include graphene oxide or graphene hydroxide. They also have nanobots and other scientifically-manufactured products designed to turn our bodies into receivers that can be connected to remotely.

Dr. Carrie Madej on Hydras and Ingredients in Bioweapon Injections
rumble.com/vn482j-dr.-carrie-madej-first-u.s.-lab-examines-vaccine-vials-horrific-findings-re.html

When we put Dr. Morgan's information on 21st century warfare tactics together with Dr. Madej's findings in the bioweapon injections, we begin to see a clearer picture. The Bolsheviks are working to kill billions of people worldwide. Those of us who manage to survive will be willfully or forcefully injected with technology that will render us incapable of controlling our own thinking and actions. We will become robotic slaves controlled by a remote-access, Internet-based management system in the clouds. All of this will be lorded over by the Bolsheviks who will have successfully created the world in their own image.

In years past, I called people who talked like this, quacks and "water-sprinklers." I said they were batty cowards who did not want to confront the real villains face-to-face. With the technology we now are certain exists, the active genocide engagement with these worldwide jabs, and the open deployment of known poisons to the masses of American people happening real time, I have to make an honest assessment. The information being presented by the doctors, scientists, and researchers with courage all point to the reality of a Jew World Order agenda. The Bolsheviks even have their proxies repeatedly announcing the implementation of this NWO agenda on a regular basis. And this new order is as real as it is bizarre.

The reality set forth in this chapter should be enough for everyone who reads it to see the evil of the Bolsheviks. But for Christians, there is one last point that should shed light on how divinely sick and perverted the Bolsheviks actually are.

For every Christian, Jesus is the way. And in a profoundly direct assessment of who the Bolsheviks are and what they represent, the Bible quotes Jesus saying to them:

"I know thy works, and tribulation, and poverty, (but thou art rich) and I know the blasphemy of them which say they are Jews, and are not, but are the synagogue of Satan." (Revelation 2:9)

"Behold, I will make them of the synagogue of Satan, which say they are Jews, and are not, but do lie; behold, I will make them to come and worship before thy feet, and to know that I have loved thee." (Revelation 3:9)

Jesus identifies the Bolsheviks as the "Synagogue of Satan." He didn't say the church, mosque, temple, or house. He said the "Synagogue of Satan." This is important because it gives us a sense of direction. Then Jesus goes on to say:

"Ye are of your father the devil, and the lusts of your father ye will do. He was a murderer from the beginning, and abode not in the truth, because there is no truth in him. When he speaketh a lie, he speaketh of his own: for he is a liar, and the father of it." (John 8:44)

This is absolutely profound. Either Jesus was prophesizing the evil of this pandemic, the Bolsheviks designed this genocide to mock the very word of Jesus, or some combination of both. Let us analyze how close this description matches today's COVID-19 pandemic reality.

Jesus calls the Bolsheviks the "Synagogue of Satan." This means they are active members of Satanic beliefs and practices. He then states they are of their father, the devil, who is Satan. Hence, Jesus is calling the Bolsheviks the children of Satan. Jesus goes on to state Satan's modus operandi: "He was a murderer from the beginning." This is exactly how we described The Fauci. The modern design comes out of NSSM 200 which is an international extermination program crafted by Kissinger. It was a murder program from the beginning.

Then Jesus says: ". . . and abode not in the truth, because there is no truth in him. When he speaketh a lie, he speaketh of his own: for he is a liar, and the father of it." The censorship that has prevented people from hearing the truth about what is going on was engineered by the entire MSM construct. They are not repeating lies they have innocently believed, but are crafting the lies and distributing them across the world. When any truthtellers present themselves, the media blocks them from gaining easy access to the public and rebukes any truth they tell. We have all witnessed this. Remember the "Disinformation Dozen." We have already discussed who owns and controls the MSM—the Bolshevik fathers of the lies.

If we continue to use the Bible as reference, it gets deeper. The first time we encounter Satan in the Bible, he comes as a snake —"serpent"—to Eve and manipulates her into taking the shot—sorry, eating the fruit. She then takes it to Adam and gets him to eat the fruit. The Bolsheviks are intentionally acting out this story and framing themselves as the serpents, who are going to innocent women and encouraging them to take these injections, which out of all of the toxins in the world are reportedly based in king cobra and krait *snake venom*.

Then, the Moderna mRNA patent has a technology in it called "Luciferase." It creates a bioluminescent imprint under the skin which glows when certain types of light are shined over it. It is a branding that holds information on the particular injection one receives. If we pay close attention to the term, it is Lucifer + Race = Lucifer's Race. In other words, this injection is rewriting your DNA code to make your body become a manufacturing plant for snake venom. We are being rewritten out of God's image, into Satan's image. They are scientifically turning us into them. Jesus said they were "of *their* father the devil." They are crafting us to become their children in the likeness of the Satan of the Bible—a snake.

Corona means "crown" as in "king" + virus means "venom" = king cobra venom.

"He causes all, both small and great, rich and poor, free and slave, to receive a mark on their right hand or on their foreheads, and that no one may buy or sell except one who has the mark or the name of the beast, or the number of his name. Here is wisdom. Let him who has understanding calculate the number of the beast, for it is the number of a man: His number is 666." (Revelation 13:16-18)

• On June 20, 2019, Microsoft Technology Licensing, LLC (Bill Gates) filed patent WO 2020/0**6**0**6**0**6** A1 for connecting people to cryptocurrency.

• On May 1, 2020, U.S. Representative Bobby L. Rush (D-IL) introduced H.R. **666**6—COVID-19 Testing, Reaching, And Contacting Everyone (TRACE) Act, forcing contact tracing, quarantines, and more.

• On February 2, 2021, U.S. Representative Ayanna S. Pressley (D-MA) introduced H.R. **666**—Anti-Racism in Public Health Act of 2021. This bill gives the U.S. government the justification to focus prioritizing the harmful injections (DNA-altering snake venom injections) to Black people over other Americans. We get to be first in line for genocide. It is presented under the guise of fighting for health equality and against police brutality.

• Pfizer's Wuhan, China office address is: Building B14, No. **666**, Gaoxin Avenue, Donghuxi njishu Development Zone Wuhan, Hubei, 430073 China

• Mask mandates: Stand 6 feet apart from the next person, 3 people in line: **6** feet **6** feet **6** feet

• ACE2 aka rs2285**666** is the genetic marker that allows people to get very sick from The Fauci. Ashkenazi Jews do not have this marker.

• A "guardian" statue displayed at the UN in New York City (November-December 2021), likened to the end-times beast from the book of Revelation, was removed.

"And the beast which I saw was like unto a leopard, and his feet were as the feet of a bear, and his mouth as the mouth of a lion: and the dragon gave him his power, and his seat, and great authority." (Revelation 13:2)

Gates was meeting with the infamous homophile Jeffrey Epstein to get funding. We believe Epstein and his Israeli funders were going to pay Gates to get Epstein's DNA and include it into upcoming bioweapon injections. In this way, everyone receiving an injection could have Epstein's pedophile DNA coded into their new DNA after the mRNA jab.

Microsoft (Bill Gates) partnered with Marina Abramovic to do an AI ad. She is a filthy, pedophilic, cannibalistic, world-renown Satanist. These injections are the 21st century AI weapon system of choice. So, Gates was working with Epstein, Abramovic, and The Fauci all at the same time. He was mixing the genocide agenda with world-renowned pedophiles and Satanic icons.

Marina Abramovic and Jacob Rothschild posing in front of "Satan Summoning His Legions" painting

Marina Abramovic

Marina Abramovic "Spirit Cooking" Dinner in 2011
bitchute.com/video/dptXK2jxMY8l

Marina Abramovic on Microsoft Artificial Intelligence Commercial in 2020
bitchute.com/video/kRaw0aXBeb8T

I bring this to your attention to show you how the Bolsheviks use symbolism. They have some type of perverse obsession with publicly announcing their assault on people. They get a kick out of watching the *goyim* suffer while the solution to their problems is put right before them. They truly believe the *goyim* are too stupid to figure this out and too cowardly to do anything about it, even if we do figure it out.

What they do not want Christians to know is that they are getting them to pledge allegiance to Satan by accepting those DNA-altering injections. This is a direct assault and the ultimate insult on Christianity. To turn lovers of Jesus Christ into some form of physical serpents that represent Satan through their DNA structure is the most wicked thing many of us have ever conceived.

The following is a brief chronological outline that highlights important dates/events leading up to The Fauci:

2005 U.S. Senator Barack Obama helps negotiate deal for U.S.-backed bioweapon laboratories in Ukraine.

2014 October 17 U.S. government enacts moratorium against funding GoFR.

2014 December 2 U.S. President Barack Obama gives a speech laying the groundwork for international delivery of vaccinations and other medical needs in the event of a global pandemic caused by a virus. He also *subtly suggests* that GoFR done by the National Institutes of Health should still be funded.

2015 Fauci goes against the moratorium and funds GoFR in a lab in Wuhan, China to see if the coronavirus in bats can be made more deadly and spread to people.

2017 December Tal Zaks, chief medical officer for Moderna, explains mRNA technology on TEDx. In it, he brags scientists are "actually hacking the software of life," enter the DNA structure, and tell the body what to do.

2019 June 20 Microsoft Technology Licensing, LLC (Bill Gates) filed patent WO 2020/060606 A1 to connect people's identities to cryptocurrency.

2019 August Cambridge University warns of biowarfare weapons targeted at specific racial groups and of AI and genetic manipulation being likely sources of world conflict.

2019 August Fort Detrick biowarfare lab was shut down by the CDC over concern a deadly bioweapon could be released and infect the planet.

2019 October The Bill & Melinda Gates Foundation partnered with Johns Hopkins Center for Health Security and the WEF to host Event 201 in New York City. They discussed what to do in case of an "unexpected" coronavirus pandemic outbreak. Among their conclusions was that they would have to implement censorship on American citizens who don't agree mass vaccination is the solution. Ten weeks later, the outbreak was announced from China.

2019 December First reported outbreaks of The Fauci in Wuhan, China.

2020 January 31 President Trump banned travel between the U.S. and China due to The Fauci.

2020 April President Trump advised the American people to use HCQ to fight The Fauci.

2020 April Fauci discourages the American public from using HCQ to fight The Fauci.

2020 April President Trump announces that African-Americans are being most effected by The Fauci and something needs to be done. ***Fauci says that nothing can be done to help African-Americans during this crisis.***

2020 May U.S. government agencies begin discouraging citizens from going to beaches and other outdoor events where they can get sunshine and vitamin D.

2020 May President John Magufuli of Tanzania exposed fake coronavirus testing process by secretly sending samples of oil, goats, fruits, etc., which came back positive for coronavirus. He embarrassed the entire Western leadership and ignored the entire pandemic scare. His nation remained open for business without restrictions. Very few Tanzanian people reportedly died from the plandemic since The Fauci was first announced in December 2019 until his murder in March 2021.

2020 December 14 The first experimental "vaccines" (harmful injections) to fight The Fauci were reportedly administered in America on that day. They were Pfizer mRNA injections.

2021 January 8 Twitter permanently bans President Trump from its platform, setting the precedent for hardcore censorship in America. This was the official launching of the war against the First Amendment to the U.S. Constitution (Amendment I).

2021 February The powerful harmful injection advocates enlist famous people with large followings to endorse the harmful injections in order to encourage the masses to get them.

2021 March Social media companies prepare for another major assault on the Amendment I by targeting all anti-injection posts for neutralization. They start removing all impactful evidence that was against the "assaxinations" (COVID-19 vaccinations).

2021 March 17 President Magufuli transitions reportedly of complications from The Fauci. He was Afrika's leading voice against the Western assaxinations. It is widely believed he was targeted and murdered by nefarious factions seeking to spread the assaxinations densely throughout the Afrikan world community.

2021 March 21 12 American citizens are identified and targeted for censorship for being the primary influencers who are informing the public on the dangers of these experimental injections.

2021 July 7 Haiti's President Jovenel Moïse was assassinated at a time when not one out of the 11 million Haitian citizens had received the harmful injection. He refused to create mandatory assaxination laws against his people.

2021 July 14 The U.S. sends 500,000 vials of Moderna assaxinations to Haiti a week after the murder of its president. These are the first harmful injections introduced to the Haitian population.

2021 July 28 President Samia Suluhu Hassan of Tanzania takes the jab and reverses everything Magufuli stood for in Tanzania. She is now advocating the assaxinations to the people of Tanzania.

2021 July 29 Biden announces more financial incentives for American citizens to get the injections and mandatory assaxinations for all federal government employees.

We have to be mindful of the fact the Bolsheviks may have successfully injected close to half the planet with The Fauci shots and plan to do even more. They have an idea on the expiration of people who have already taken the injection; we do not. Remember, it took an estimated 25 years or so for Hilary Koprowski's vaccine injections to kill our Brothers and Sisters in Afrika. That was quickly blamed on something called AIDS. The Bolsheviks have had 35 years to perfect the effects of these time-delayed injections.

This means we actually have no idea what is in store for the *goyim* in terms of delayed rates of death among our populations or mass sterilization amongst our youth. If we are lucky, it will not be as cataclysmic as we might presume. If they are working their plan well, we must brace for a time-delayed collision with a genocide of massive proportions.

It could come in two years. It could come in 10 years. It could come in 20 or 30 years. It may never come. But we would be wise to deal with the Bolsheviks now while we have the kind of numbers that give us an advantage.

In concluding this chapter, we must be clear the "COVID-19 pandemic" stage of WWIII is only the beginning. Starvation, police terrorism, intensified racial hostility, severely restricted travel, economic strangulation, AI injections, normalized pedophilia in schools, bestiality, broadly promoted Satanic worship and practice, global warfare, more severe lockdowns, false incarceration, escalated organ trafficking, normalized cannibalism, etc., are all on the way.

What will slow this massive genocide? This book of course. As it spreads throughout the world, people will be forced to investigate the claims herein. They will not only find it to be true; but the situation is far worse than stated. This book is the first step towards turning the tide on the Bolsheviks.

On the next page are suggested products for general health and to detox the body from these bioweapon injections. **We are particularly favorable towards the NAC (N-acetyl Cysteine) supplement.** It has been credited with stopping the replication of spike protein and effectively detoxifying cells.

BOLSHEVIKS ARE THE PROBLEM!

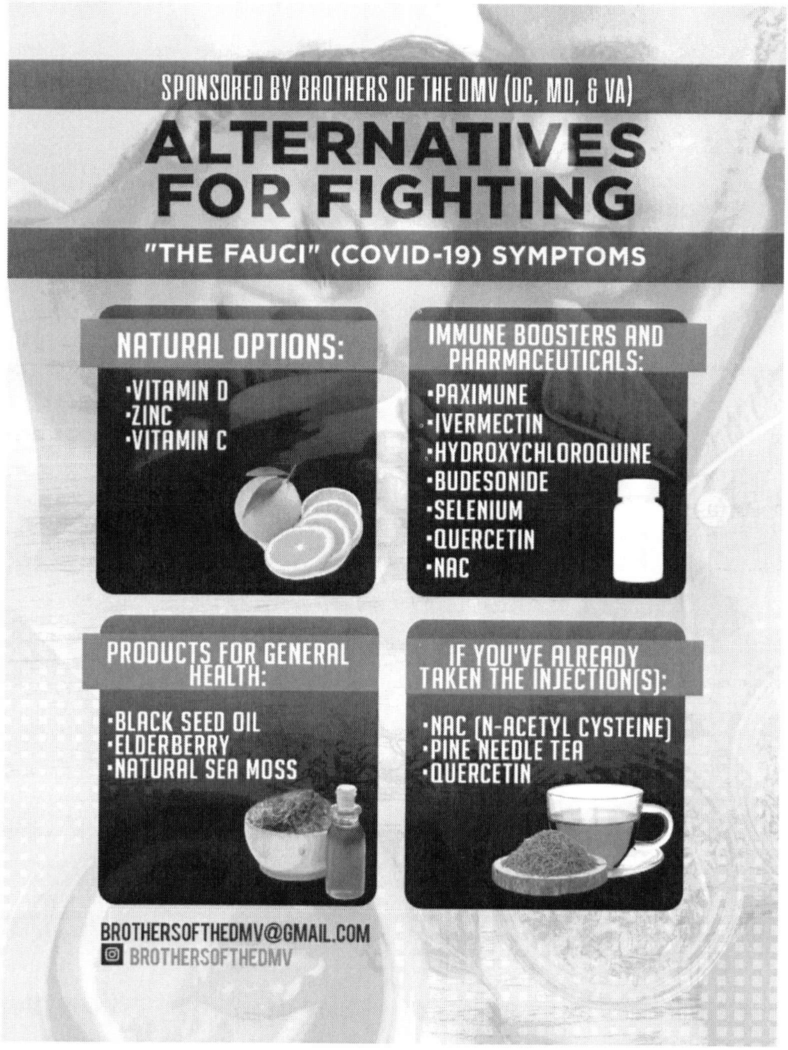
SPONSORED BY BROTHERS OF THE DMV (DC, MD, & VA)
ALTERNATIVES FOR FIGHTING
"THE FAUCI" (COVID-19) SYMPTOMS
NATURAL OPTIONS:
•VITAMIN D
•ZINC
•VITAMIN C
IMMUNE BOOSTERS AND PHARMACEUTICALS:
•PAXIMUNE
•IVERMECTIN
•HYDROXYCHLOROQUINE
•BUDESONIDE
•SELENIUM
•QUERCETIN
•NAC
PRODUCTS FOR GENERAL HEALTH:
•BLACK SEED OIL
•ELDERBERRY
•NATURAL SEA MOSS
IF YOU'VE ALREADY TAKEN THE INJECTION(S):
•NAC (N-ACETYL CYSTEINE)
•PINE NEEDLE TEA
•QUERCETIN
BROTHERSOFTHEDMV@GMAIL.COM
BROTHERSOFTHEDMV

6

MAKE IT PLAIN

We are writing this book to save the world from Bolshevik extermination, not to prove how scholastic we can be. As a result, this book is being written with haste. It is designed to enlighten and push people to direct action. Throughout the previous chapters, we have done our best to make a solid case, with sufficient references, on our position that the Bolsheviks are the problem on this planet. From this point forward, we will talk directly to the people.

The Bolsheviks have attacked and attempted to commit genocide against every race on this planet. Levy Andrew helped procure the blankets with smallpox for British General Sir Jeffrey Amherst to exterminate Pontiac's Native American Alliance army. This extermination led to the birth of America. The Sassoon family launched the Opium Wars against China for their own financial benefit, destroying millions of Chinese lives in the process. Bolsheviks controlled the wealth of South Africa and dominated the Apartheid system. The Oppenheimer and De Beers families are still exploiting the wealth of Afrika to this day. The opioid crisis in America was manufactured by the Bolshevik Sackler family. They destroyed over 500,000 U.S. families and were found guilty in court. They have faced no criminal time for their assault on the people of this Republic. So, we can see both history and the modern day demonstrate major drug addiction and the destruction of family and culture, is a direct result of Bolshevik tyranny.

The Transatlantic Slave Trade, the world's most horrifying holocaust, was conceived, managed, and controlled by the Bolsheviks. They are directly responsible for why Afrikan people are in the Western Hemisphere in the numbers we are today.

During one of the many assaults on Palestinians, the Bolsheviks (Israelis) took control of the media and locked down the entire region. No one could leave their homes. They only allowed one television station to air and they played XXX pornography on it 24/7. In order for the Palestinians to get updates, the only form of communication available was the television. In order to watch the television, they had to endure hardcore pornography all day and night. What kind of beasts are these Bolsheviks? People were under military siege, uncertain if they or their family would live another day, and these beasts forced mothers and fathers to play pornography around children in order to get any information.

[Author's note: Every race has a pogrom sponsored by the Bolsheviks they consider the worst holocaust of all time. If we allow them to succeed in this WWIII battle of extermination, we can stop the debate. This holocaust will be a DNA holocaust that will be the worst tragedy in the history of the world. We all lose. The Bolsheviks win. We must not allow this to happen.]

In January 2015, Malaysian Prime Minister Mahathir Mohamad stated "Jews rule the world by proxy." Henry Ford said the International Jew was the world's foremost problem. Martin Luther, the Great Reformer, was so disgusted with their behavior, some credit him with helping formulate Adolf Hitler's philosophy.

If ever we had enough courage to release the bondage of Bolshevik intellectual tyranny, we would read *Mein Kampf* and learn more about what made Hitler move in the direction he did. One chapter in particular will move any socio-politically aware American citizen with an open mind. Chapter XI, called "Nation and Race," reads like someone breaking down the George Soros-funded LGBT BLM/JAM and Antifa protests over the past few years. I actually had to verify I had the original text. He brilliantly laid down the modus operandi of the Bolsheviks such that one can understand why they have marked him as the pariah of world history. This chapter alone is chilling and worth the read for anyone wanting to know what to expect from Bolsheviks. It reads like it was literally written five years ago about what is going on here in America today.

Bolsheviks are the driving force behind all of the major social ills in the world today. They control and promote:

1) Feminism (female hatred of men, the intellectual expression of lesbianism)
2) Homophilia
3) Pornography
4) Censorship
5) Drug addiction (Sackler family financed the opioid crisis in America)
6) Misogyny (hip-hop culture)
7) Mass incarceration
8) Food shortages
9) Homelessness
10) Effeminization of America's men
11) Chronic divorce
12) Dysfunctional school system where youth are barely learning
13) Drug trafficking
14) Organ trafficking
15) Human trafficking

They have dismantled America and stripped it naked. They disassembled and decentralized America's production capacity and pushed producers out of the country. They also cheapened the quality of jobs available for American citizens.

The Bolsheviks launched a strategic war against America's defense with The Fauci. When they began administering the harmful injections, they targeted four major groups:

1) Military (who provide national security)
2) Healthcare professionals (who heal the troops & U.S. citizens)
3) Teachers (who nurture and cultivate the minds of future generations)
4) Government employees (who manage and administer the infrastructure and logistics for the nation)

If we look closely at these groups, we recognize The Fauci as an organized military assault on America with the objective of bringing the Republic to its knees. This is precisely where the country currently is—on its knees. The Bolsheviks targeted the core of national defense in America and are preparing for the full collapse of the U.S. Republic.

White Folks—Stop Being Blockheads!

They are also using White America's Achilles' heel. The hundreds of years of American hatred for Black people standing on thousands of years of Hamitic Myth indoctrination makes Anglo-Saxons easily ignitable to attack, harm, and kill Black people. It is the No. 1 tool in the arsenal of Bolsheviks in America. Whenever they get close to being exposed and targeted, they always sponsor some type of racial unrest. The easiest and most effective of their tactics is to use White violence against Black people as the catalyst for social disruption. They generally do this in either one of three ways:

1) A person with a Bolshevik last name harms or murders an innocent Black person: George **Zimmerman** killed Trayvon Martin. If his name was Pedro Martinez, White America would not have supported him. But with his Bolshevik name, he posed as an everyday conservative White American patriot. He enlisted White support from FOX News, militias, White supremacist groups, law enforcement, media personalities, and everyday White folks. The Anglo-Saxon masses were then encouraged to either join the side of the murderer or join the Bolshevik-sponsored Black liberal gaytards who express Bolshevik liberal talking points.

The angry masses of Black people who are truly outraged at this genocidal process are muffled and barely ever heard. We are only shown to the public when our outcry for justice reaches the point of physical demonstration. Sincere Black people on the ground end up fighting against the racist White supporters of Bolshevik Talmudic-styled torture and murder of Black people, law enforcement who defend Bolshevik Talmudic torture and murder of Black people, mainstream Bolshevik media that puts LGBT agenda mouthpieces in positions to falsely represent our outrage, Black-skinned/White-masked Black people who are mouthpieces for either White conservative or liberal talking points, and the actual criminal who assaulted or killed our kindred.

Neither Black nor Anglo-Saxon people ever think to take control of the narrative and ask, "Why does a man with a definitively Jewish name chase down a 17-year-old Black teenager and murder him?

This sounds like something from the Babylonian Talmud where it is permitted to randomly murder Gentiles. He had no right to murder that young man because that behavior is un-American."

The torture and murder of George Floyd by Derek Chauvin and the ramming a plunger handle in the rectum of Abner Louima by Justin Volpe, follow the same or similar pattern discussed above.

2) An Anglo-Saxon harms or murders an innocent Black person: Michael Brown and Sandra Bland. White Anglo-Saxons rally behind the White murderer and defend the heinous genocidal act and become willing accomplices to the crime. The Bolshevik media either ignores the abuse and/or runs it repeatedly in order to fuel racial unrest. They show the Anglo-Saxon (72%) and Black (9%)-run police forces supporting our genocide across the airwaves and wait for our response. The Bolsheviks then use this distraction to implement and/or push some agenda they have which has little to nothing to do with the crime committed.

Black people become rightfully embittered and view White folks as devils with no hearts who love celebrating, justifying, and participating in the torture and murder of Black men, women, and children. We begin to truly consider whether White folks are "human" with the way they justify and support our destruction. The racial hatred sinks deeper into our hearts and we secretly long for the day when White brutality is brought to an end, no matter what the cost.

3) Some Bolshevik takes a real or imaginary violation of a White woman by a Black man and promotes it to the world as a historical burning desire of Black men to rape White women. This is usually done through media. Whites become enraged and begin systematically attacking Black people throughout the country under the notion of protecting their women. The original claims are most often fabricated or exaggerated to get the desired Bolshevik result.

These are the primary three ways Bolsheviks use White hatred of Black people to keep racial conflict brewing. This racial conflict is the proverbial "get out of jail free" card for the Bolsheviks. Whenever they get exposed for being the monsters they are, this is the card they pull: the race card. And it does not only work on White folks. Whenever they want to attack Anglo-Saxons, they simply turn on the replay button of all the crimes Anglo-Saxons have committed, or Bolsheviks posing as Anglo-Saxons committed, against Black people and use it against White folks.

For instance, take the breakdown above and let us examine the 2020 election theft. Since 1996, Black people have been privy to FOX News openly supporting the decimation of the Black race. They routinely and religiously express hatred and vitriol for Black people. Their anchors are made up of middle-American White patriotic types who are clearly Anglo-Saxon. Bill O'Reilly, Sean Hannity, Tucker Carlson, Brian Kilmeade, etc. From a Black perspective, all of them represent the face of overt "racism White supremacy" in America. They feel to us like the modern-day version of a sophisticated KKK. The baseline of consensus is that it is OK for police to brutalize and murder Black people, and they boldly defend this behavior on a regular basis.

Their racist behavior is so blatant it cannot be denied. I watched Kilmeade airing a program on the effects of these injections on White teenagers. Instead of being outraged at the Bolshevik assault on Anglo-Saxon youth, he asks the U.S. government to send these "needed" injections to Nigeria, Somalia, Uganda, Norway, or Japan. He threw Norway in near the end so the racist overtones would be missed. They were not. This is the very definition of the psychopathic racial personality. What I heard in my mind was: "Kill the Black people. And the Asians can be killed as well. But please stop killing our children, Mr. Bolshevik." That is exactly how I interpreted his comments. A real man would say: "We have to stop these shots altogether because they are harmful." But begging the Bolsheviks to continue the genocide against Black people is far safer for a coward than confronting the Bolsheviks for their crimes against your people.

What White folks do not realize is FOX News was not designed for them to have an open space to share their conservative views. It was created to use them as proxy agents of Black genocide in America, so when the Bolsheviks decided to openly overthrow the

Republic, Black people would identify the White conservatives as the aggressors and bad guys. Of course, we would not be wise enough to recognize what is really going on. We would simply be happy to see anything that hurt the FOX News network anchors and everyone who supports them in America. So, when it was time for Arizona to be called in the 2020 election and FOX News prematurely announced Biden as the winner, it was clear to those of us with vision that Trump was so far ahead in the election the Bolsheviks had to pull out all the stops. They showed their hand. They own and control FOX News and the fix was in. They were going to steal the election because Trump won by such a large margin the preset electronic ballet booth algorithms did not compensate enough to steal the election for Biden.

Where did Black people fit in? We were the proxy agents for our own destruction. We were proxied to assist in the ballot theft in each of the swing states. We proudly took the challenge to fight racist White America and the evil President Trump represented. Even though he financially supported Historically Black Colleges and Universities, was open to prison reform, and suggested we use HCQ which would have saved us from the luciferase, somehow, he was Lucifer. In reality, he did represent racist White America and anti-Black sentiment in this country, even if these were not his personal sentiments. Hence, though our people were wrong to support the ballot fraud, FOX News provided the fuel. Why wouldn't we hate people who routinely justify our murder? The truth is terrorism from law enforcement and the general White populace was destined to uptick if Trump won the 2020 election. However, we would not have been facing forced injection mandates or masks. Nor would we be this close on the landslide towards global genocide. In other words, we had to "pick our poison." Many of us picked wrong.

The reality is that the limited Black participation in the ballot fraud was negligible. More Black people voted for Trump in 2020 than in 2016. In this regard, he actually won the Black vote. He split the Hispanic vote 50/50. And he dominated the White vote. Trump won the election hands down, despite all the election fraud. The Bolsheviks just decided to boldly stop counting the ballots on election night and change the entire outcome the next day in front of the world. We all witnessed it. But most Black people were happy to see the devout racists at FOX News who represent the sentiment of the Trump base take the loss, regardless of how it happened.

Smallhats: Mortal Enemies to Planet Earth **(3-DVD Set)**
Including Disc 2: "Whole Stole the 2020 Election?"
Electronic Email Download MP4 Version
socialarchitects26.com/Smallhats-Mortal-Enemy-to-Planet-Earth-3-Disc-DVD-Set-mp4-Electronic-Email-Version-p279862011

So even though it was 100% Bolshevik-sponsored and-organized, the 2020 election theft was conveniently left at the foot of Black people in the swing states. This was done so if Trump's administration or the Anglo-Saxons in America forced an investigation or took direct action against the stolen election, the Bolsheviks could easily use the media footage to make Black people in America the sacrificial lambs for slaughter. Black people were strategically positioned to be the scapegoats for the 2020 election theft if it became necessary.

Trump did not lose the election because of any racial group. Nor did he lose because of any political party. He did not lose because he did not lose. He won the election. But his family, cabinet, and administration were littered with Bolsheviks. You could not even talk to President Trump without going through Jared Kushner. Since the Bolsheviks were the ones overthrowing the election, his only option to claim his victory was to activate the Insurrection Act of 1807. He did not have the guts nor the support system to effectively accomplish this task; and as a result, he had his victory taken from him.

The striking thing about these FOX News anchors is they are utter cowards. With all of the tough guy, hardline antics they tend to portray, they *never* criticize the Bolsheviks or Israel. These cowards did not even mention the Bolsheviks when their own network called

Arizona for Biden and stole the election. They do not mention the Bolsheviks when they criticize the bioweapon injections. They ignore the Bolshevik's push for war with Russia, or Israel's neutral stance in this cold war against Russia.

The primary point I am making is White folks have to stop being blockheads and cowards. As long as Anglo-Saxons operate as proxies for Bolshevik aggression and oppression of Black people, we can never get close enough to the Bolsheviks to have any impact. Black people spend every day in this country living under the threat of random kneejerk racial aggression from White America. Hence, White folks are our overseers. And our overseers have overseers: The Bolsheviks. If White folks in America would stop being braindead, simpleminded puppets for the Bolsheviks, maybe we could wake up the braindead, simpleminded Black puppets to who the Bolsheviks really are. But until White America releases its knees off of the necks of Black people and learns to control their emotions, we will be locked in a battle with them for our survival, as the Bolsheviks continue to exterminate both groups.

[Author's note: It is worth mentioning here that Black people are not the only proxies used against Anglo-Saxons. The creation of the spike protein (GoFR-engineered snake poison) occurred in the U.S. GoFR to launch the pandemic was conceived, financed, requested, and supported in the U.S. Fauci and the NIAID financed China in completing the research; but China did not create the technology for The Fauci. Somehow, Americans are blaming China for a plandemic where the dry run occurred in New York City 10 weeks before it began. *Event 201 did not take place in China!* China has simply been positioned as the fall guy in case American citizens start honing in too closely on the role of the Bolsheviks in this crisis. The MSM will simply spin the narrative towards the "Chinese Virus Pandemic."

Everyone will fall on board with the narrative and start discussing nuking China like FOX News anchors discuss nuking President Putin now. The Bolsheviks pull our strings and we dance to their tune.

When we saw Mark Zuckerberg with a Chinese mate, that should have alerted us to this scheme. It should be clear to all that this newfound wealthy Bolshevik attraction for Asians is part of the program to totally collapse America and make China a competitor for the world superpower position. Yes, the Bolsheviks are in China heavy, pulling some strings.]

When China Sneezes: From the Coronavirus Lockdown to the Global Politico-Economic Crisis by Dr. Cynthia McKinney
amazon.com/When-China-Sneezes-Coronavirus-Politico-Economic/dp/1949762246

Black Folks—Stop Being Blockheads!

My people are in a very difficult situation. We are fighting a multitude of real battles while simultaneously facing an apocalyptic chemical/biological genocide. We face constant Anglo-Saxon aggression, police aggression, perverse culture addiction, job discrimination, economic oppression, LGBT curriculum assault, chronic pedophilia, pandemic homosexuality, fatherless homes, toxic feminism, a tragic identity crisis, and many more issues. Almost every ill we face can be traced back to some evil Bolshevik scheme.

[Author's note: It is eerie whenever I begin research on some aspect of racial oppression of Black people. Invariably, while trying to cling to a White racist narrative, I stumble across some Bolshevik who either contributed significantly, funded it, expanded it, started it, or conceived it. They are heavily invested in the oppression of Black people around the world.]

Our most courageous, intelligent, and sophisticated freedom fighters always pointed out the evil of the Bolsheviks. Some of them were well known for physically confronting these death monsters. For instance, Dr. Khalid Abdul Muhammad is reported to have singlehandedly knocked out one of the leaders of the JDL—Jewish Defense League—when they were the most feared Bolshevik group in the U.S. During a speech at Kean College in New Jersey in the 1990s, Dr. Muhammad gave a scathing criticism of Bolshevik behavior. The Bolsheviks ran to the government and convinced the U.S. Congress to censor Muhammad. This was another case where an enemy of the Bolshevik was fought by the Anglo-Saxon proxy foot soldiers. The Jews could not have accomplished this without complicity from Anglo-Saxon and some Black members in Congress.

In Muhammad's case, I am more disappointed in Black people's behavior than anyone else's. We had one of the most prolific figures in Black American history fighting the leaders of this demonic group. He actually laid one to sleep on the concrete. This is the definition of a Black man. But in the prime of his life, he was struggling to maintain his momentum partly due to financial constraints. This problem was initiated by another reality.

Bolsheviks try to economically castrate all serious threats. In the Black community, they have neutralized almost all outspoken, strong, consistent Black voices who identify them as a problem. They have taken economic control of our schools, churches (through government grants), intellectuals, scholars, lecturers, businesses, politicians, and government programs to fund social efforts. They control our television programming, our school curriculums, our cultural expression, and many of the leaders of Afrikan nations. So, when it comes time to support authentic Black leadership like Muhammad, we do not have enough people with the economic stability, self-sufficiency, and courage to do so.

The most valuable asset to the Black community they have taken control over is our women. To a large and unhealthy degree, our women have become the walking, breathing, thinking, and acting proxy agents for the Bolsheviks. Whatever disastrous agenda the Bolsheviks seek to push on Black people, we can expect it to be championed by Black women today. Pedophilia, homosexuality, transgenderism, interracial relationships, hatred of Black men, injection mandates, lesbianism, feminism, etc., are things Black women *never* supported. The Bolsheviks have mastered the art of turning Black women against the interests of their own race and their own men. This becomes an incredibly difficult situation to navigate, as it pits the group against itself. In fact, in some ways, it is easier to fight Anglo-Saxon proxy wars than Black relationship proxy wars.

With Black leaders and many Black women worldwide controlled by Bolsheviks, it is very easy to lead Black people in the wrong direction. When the "Justice for Mike Brown" movement was taken over by the Bolshevik-controlled, George Soros-funded, LGBT-promoting, Gay Lesbian Movement (formerly known as BLM), the battle was won. Billionaire Bolsheviks pay Black homophiles and lesbians to make a few television appearances at rallies and blasted it throughout their media. They paid them to fly around the country and steal the momentum of genuine movements and crush the voices of the real warriors like Daren Seales in Ferguson. By the time the Bolsheviks were finished, you had an entire movement limp, millions of dollars of donations from well-meaning people spent on mansions and other accessories for a group of obnoxious queers, and a "Black uprising" that changed focus from justice to the perpetrator into "burn it down and destroy the buildings so Bolshevik investors can return and purchase the properties at alarmingly low prices." Many genuine activist movements start off as rebellions against abuse and turn into Bolshevik land grabs.

The crisis is in our leadership and our organization. If a White nationalist or a non-White foreigner was looking for a known grassroots Afrikan-American activist who was against Zionism or the Bolsheviks, most Black people would have no idea where to start looking. This leaves the Black community, who is traditional and conservative by nature, following the Bolshevik pied piper melody of self-destruction: "Be gay is the way," "Get the jab and make sure your booster has a booster."

Because there is almost no tangible anti-Bolshevik understanding and energy in the Black community, it leaves our people in a perpetual state of proxy to be battering rammed into Anglo-Saxon Americans at the simple bequest of the Bolshevik. There is no voice to tell our people to maintain our course and stay away from the slippery Bolsheviks and their blood money.

As a result of this reality, our people are just as susceptible to being rammed into Anglo-Saxons as they are into us. The difference is our proxy wars do not generally result in dead White folks. Their proxy wars generally result in dead Black folks.

Our situation is exacerbated now that the most relevant voices in the Black community do not have a simple means to communicate with the masses. Censorship on social media changed the general way serious dialog is exchanged online, and we have not created the necessary tools to replace Facebook, Twitter, and YouTube. As a result, mature Black discourse is restricted to the privacy of chat groups and local organizational activity. This type of organization is great; but it does not fully compensate for what is missing.

This book is designed to demonstrate Black people's capacity to affect the current world situation and demonstrate it through literature. Members of other races will get to meet the type of Black personalities they do not even imagine exist. They will have a place to reach out and dialog with people who are not interested in social integration, but who do want to fix the problem. We grow food, we protect family culture, and we shoot back. Anyone who can respect these qualities will have a place to connect with the real Black community.

As if the Bolsheviks were preparing for this book to be released, in April 2022 they used their power in Western Israel to try to officially bring an end to Amendment 1. Bolshevik U.S. Secretary of Homeland Security, Alejandro Mayorkas, appointed Bolshevik Nina Jankowicz as the executive director of a newly created department, the Disinformation Governance Board (DGB). This department was created for one purpose. The Bolsheviks know the American people are catching on to them. It is only a matter of time before a resource like *Jews Are The Problem* is released to the American Republic. My right as an American citizen to publicly release this book and share this life-saving information with the American people will be in direct conflict with the Bolshevik overthrow of Amendment I and the American Republic. They will not be able to ignore it and they will make a decision to attack me, the author.

I will ***never***—and neither should you—comply to being a citizen of Western Israel. For what it is worth, I am an Afrikan with American citizenship and I will stand on the Constitution in the face of Bolshevik tyranny. I consider the creation of the DGB an act of overt sedition to the U.S. Constitution and I will not support this Bolshevik overthrow of the Republic. Whatever the cost, it is worth it to me. I only get one life and I will always live it and die it a Black Man.

Black people, we must get these Bolsheviks out of our minds, our pockets, and our bedrooms. Their undesired presence in the construct of our social lives is killing us. And we are no good to our men, women, or children if we cannot drive them out of our race by any means possible. Dr. Tony Martin told us this years ago. Today we are in a situation where our very lives depend on it.

Conclusion

White folks, you need to chill out on Black people and stop being cowards with these Bolsheviks. They are publicly committing genocide against your race. You are losing your genetic lives. You must begin to call them out. Stand by those who call them out and start strategically dodging Bolshevik proxy wars with Black people. Many of us share reservations about trusting and working with one another, and that is understood. At the same time, we must learn not to engage in unnecessary hostility with one another in the interest of our collective survival. Tell your police officers to focus on the 100,000 Ukrainian Bolsheviks who are flooding this country in preparation for the 21st century Bolshevik Revolution (military invasion to take your guns) and leave us alone. If we have to fight one another, there will be no one strong enough to fight the Bolsheviks when they are ready for the full-on attack of the Republic.

BOLSHEVIKS ARE THE PROBLEM!

7

WHAT WE MUST DO TO STOP GLOBAL GENOCIDE

The Bolsheviks have declared open warfare on the "software of life," DNA. This means all non-Bolsheviks are facing slavery and/or extermination. In fact, their form of slavery where DNA codes have been permanently restructured through mRNA technology, is technically slavery and genocide. They killed the old person to enslave the new type of person.

In this war, there are only two sides:

1) Bolsheviks and their Proxies
2) The Rest of Us

The Bolsheviks are only offering us slavery or genocide as options. We have not accepted these terms and offered ours. In fact, if we view this as a war, we must take a practical look at the casualty rate for each team.

It is reasonable to conclude with the worldwide deaths from the released bioweapon, lack of appropriate medical treatment, administration of poison, depression, suicide, adverse events from the injection bioweapon, murder of leaders of countries who resisted the injection war, etc., the Bolsheviks have tallied up at least 1 million casualties on The Rest of Us.

To date, I believe The Rest of Us have tallied up a whopping zero on the casualty scoreboard for the Bolsheviks and their Proxies.

If The Rest of Us want to survive, we will have to up these numbers. Who would join a war on the side of righteousness with these odds? No intelligent person would. We have to change the way we view this war and make it more practical. So, what do we do?

1) Agree interracial dating and marriage are a source for contention among Black and Anglo-Saxon men. We will agree not to participate in, promote, or endorse such behavior as we both see it as suicidal for our people.
2) White police officers will retarget their hatred and aggression towards the Bolsheviks and away from Black people. This will allow us the necessary breathing room to prepare for this undertaking.
3) Open, constant dialogue between pro-Black and pro-Anglo groups of men who are ready to stand up and fight for our survival. We are not meeting to become buddies. We are both being slaughtered by the same bad guys. **Ban Bolsheviks from these discussions!**
4) White folks must stop viewing the Bolshevik as your brothers and sisters. Unless they are Cain and you wish to be Abel, the Bolsheviks are always Bolsheviks. Stop being their proxies.
5) We must collectively strip them of their title of "God's Chosen People." This provides them tremendous latitude to destroy. From now on, we will collectively refer to them as either Bolsheviks, the Synagogue of Satan, or Smallhats.
6) We will stop referring to Jesus Christ as a "Jew." He was the Son of God according to the scriptures, not a Jew. He was the "King of the Jews" and they killed him because they would not conform to decent behavior. We will collectively view them as the killers of Jesus and all that is righteous, even if we are not ourselves Christians.
7) We agree not to comply with the homophile agenda, period. No more homo promo.

If we can agree on these simple terms of engagement, we can begin discussions immediately. There is no reason that mature Black men and Anglo-Saxon men cannot sit at a table and discuss this crisis, including our points of agreement and our points of disagreement. We can discuss survival. Most of all, we can work on our numbers!

Once we develop effective working relationships between White and Black groups committed to ending Bolshevik hegemony,

Bolsheviks will start presenting deals. They will apologize for the overreach and offer Anglo-Saxons the opportunity to join them in the annihilation of Black people worldwide. They will use their leverage to push China into a war with the West or host a Beijing Conference mirroring the Berlin Conference for the pillaging of the Afrikan continent. Perhaps they will attack Russia directly, forcing the Russian Bear into an all-out traditional WWIII. They might even approach Black people with a partnership offer to destroy "racism White supremacy." They could present any combination of these as well.

If The Rest of Us are to engage these monsters successfully, we must agree up front to scrap all discussions with the Bolsheviks. **NO NEGOTIATIONS!**

According to Rabbi Aron Moss, in *Israel National News*, on July 25, 2006: "Every Jew is an Ambassador for Israel." We are going to have to hold them to that premise.

I will here provide limited insight into the engagement process. We are organizing to stop global genocide by a hostile foreign entity that wishes to topple the Republic and steal its sovereignty. They are also involved in premeditated acts of genocide. As a result, we as American citizens must exercise our Amendment 1 and 2 rights to save the Republic. This includes:

1) Classifying all Bolsheviks as agents of hostile foreign interests to include the Greater Israel.
2) Removing all Bolsheviks from all U.S. government positions as they are agents of hostile foreign interests.
3) Systematically targeting all harmful injections for failure from their point of manufacture—destroy these poisons at origin!
4) Making illegal organ harvesting and child-sex trafficking punishable by death by firing squad—internationally.
5) Making organized citizens arrests by militias and seizing the properties, businesses, and farmlands of all Bolsheviks and their proxies who are involved in depopulation efforts.
6) Liquidating all lands, monies, property, and other forms of wealth from the Bolsheviks and their proxies, and splitting it 50/50 Anglo and Black. Americans will once again experience prosperity. We will reconstruct

this country in a way that each group will be self-sufficient and bring value to the Republic.

7) American citizens, companies, and institutions should draft agreements and/or treaties with one another as part of an overarching set of guidelines and principles that mirror the U.S. Constitution. Here we can agree to protect the sovereignty of this nation and not to allow any foreign interests to overthrow the rights granted to all American citizens. We will essentially be cementing our citizenship and covenant with the U.S. Constitution and authorizing ourselves to create legislation to protect our rights under the Constitution. By doing this, we put tremendous pressure on the elected officials. This is but one step from U.S. citizens discarding the treasonous acts of cowardly legislators and doing it for ourselves. They will have to either quickly shape up or watch themselves be steamrolled and made irrelevant by the power of the people who are the government of the American Republic.
8) *Permanently Defund Israel and declare it to be a hostile foreign interest to the United States of America.*
9) Demand audits of the Federal Reserve and the Internal Revenue Service and aggressively pursue criminal consequences and full compensation from all entities found to have stolen from U.S. coffers.

This is very practical and achievable. It would just have to be worked out. And it does not have to take long. We can agree on three basic rules of enemy engagement:

1) No rape
2) No torture
3) No mercy

Our job is to collectively stop the global genocide of The Rest of Us and bring a final end to Bolshevik terrorism of peoples on this planet. They started a global extermination war. It is now our turn to come together and determine what our terms of warfare are. What do we want in the end?

I am in no way discounting the great work many people are doing to educate people on what is really going on. Everyone's work is greatly appreciated. We need defensive efforts to keep enough of us healthy and alive to wage this war. I wrote this chapter from the offensive side of the board. We need to continue the great defense with current and breaking information regularly; but I believe we also must accept their declaration of war and begin to fight back offensively.

Right now, the Bolsheviks have nothing to lose. They keep attacking and we keep defending. It is past time they face an offensive that forces them to defend themselves. ***This is the way.*** When we identify them with straightforward honesty and aggression, and refuse negotiations, we will realize they are few. They are wise; but they are few. Once we maneuver their proxies out of position, they are even fewer. They have no defense. They are ready to be stopped. And identifying and targeting them is the only way. No weapon is ever the problem. The person with evil intentions who wields the weapon is always the problem. We must deal with the problem.

BOLSHEVIKS ARE THE PROBLEM!

8

COWARDS SHUT UP JEWS ARE THE PROBLEM!

Anybody who tries to cover up the evil of this group is a coward. Bolsheviks are killing the entire world and very few people are willing to speak up about it. That is because the Bolsheviks have managed to turn everyone into cowards. I will not be a coward. I will die a man. And in my world, one cannot be a man and a coward at the same time.

I am sick to my stomach with cowardice in the modern world. I watch experts in disseminating information intentionally avoid identifying the Bolsheviks as the problem. I view hours of videos from experts who discuss this crisis and only the Anglo-Saxon women have the courage to identify the Bolsheviks as the problem. It is disgusting! Some of the men are clear on who is doing this; but they are cowards.

If 100 of the most popular doctors and scientists came out and identified the Bolsheviks as the problem, we could break through the fear. We could end censorship. We could expose the Bolsheviks for who and what they are. We could get the average person to say these people are evil and must be stopped. We could actually open the floodgates of justice on these demons. However, the males are too scared.

Since there are not enough men brave enough to do it in a way that it reaches the public in clear terms, I have written this book. Now, you can spread this word to everyone. Buy it. Share it. It's your Constitutional right. **Stop being a coward.** Purchase multiple copies and give them away to police officers, fraternities and sororities, lodges, churches, federal government workers, construction workers, doctors, scientists, schools, homies, love interests, fighters, leaders, followers, military personnel, athletes, etc. Everyone must have the chance to know and understand who we are fighting against. Our people perish because of a lack of knowledge.

If anyone gives you any static about possessing or reading this book, please respond in the following ways:

1) A nuisance person you do not like: "Irritated Genie said Cowards Shut Up—*Jews Are The Problem!*"
2) A friend who you do not want to offend: "I know you are not a coward. You just have not read the book yet."
3) An elder you respect: "No sir. No ma'am. He was not calling you a coward. He was talking about the other people."
4) Random cowards: "Shut up coward, *Jews Are The Problem!*"

We have to break the cognitive dissonance. We cannot survive by continuing to pretend like we do not know who is doing this. We know. Now we will act.

This conflict with the Bolsheviks will not end peacefully under any circumstances. The faster we move, the less time they have to master AI to deploy robots and other technology for our destruction. We do not want to be fighting mechanical dogs and drones when we would be more effective and efficient fighting Bolsheviks.

If we organize ourselves properly during 2023, we will be able to move aggressively towards the beginning of a resolution in 2024. This is achievable and only requires us to take our survival seriously. We will have to survive massive death cycles due to the harmful injections and other biowarfare attacks, radiation assaults, financial depression, hunger wars, etc. But if we organize now and prepare for a modern General Orders #11, we can save this planet from certain destruction.

I'll See You on the Battlefield!

BOLSHEVIKS ARE THE PROBLEM!

BOLSHEVIKS ARE THE PROBLEM!

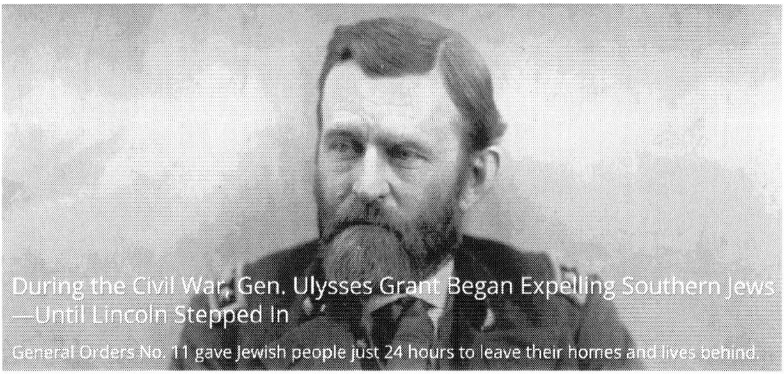

General Orders, No. 11.
HDQRS. 13TH A.C. DEPT OF THE TENN.,
Holly Springs, December 17, 1862.

The Jews, as a class violating every regulation of trade established by the Treasury Department, and also department orders, are hereby expelled from the Department within twenty-four hours from the receipt of this order.

By order of Maj. Gen. U.S. Grant:
JNO. A. RAWLINS,
Assistant Adjutant-General.

Recommended Reading List

- *Exposing the Lies of History* by Reed T. Sainsbury
- *Synagogue of Satan* by Andrew Carrington Hitchcock
- *The International Jew* by Henry Ford
- *The Jewish Onslaught* by Dr. Tony Martin
- *The Secret Relationship Between Blacks and Jews* (Volumes I-III) by NOI Research Department
- *When China Sneezes* by Dr. Cynthia McKinney

Recommended DVDs on the Bolsheviks

- *Deep State vs. White Nationalism* (2-DVD Set)
- *Fauci & the Gateway* (4-DVD Set)
- *Pizzagate: The New Slave Trade* (3-DVD Set)
- *Smallhats: Mortal Enemy to Planet Earth* (3-DVD Set)

ABOUT THE AUTHOR

Ayo H. Kimathi is a social architect who focuses on Afrikan survival in the 21st century and beyond. Social Architecture is the science of envisioning and designing a desired social environment and social order for specific families, communities, and/or nations. It requires an assessment of the undesired and most desired set of social behaviors one wants to address. It then calls for the creation of an active, achievable plan of action to remove unwanted behaviors and support the most desired behaviors in a manner that transitions them from socially engineered behaviors into established and accepted culture.

socialarchitects26.com
empowerment@socialarchitects26.com
(202) 641-1766

Stay tuned for the next edition of this book coming in the near future . . .

JEWS ARE THE PROBLEM II: THE EXPULSIONS

Menkhepera Tehudimes (Thutmose III)